FINANCIALLY FREE!

WINDWARD
PRESS

FINANCIALLY FREE!

The "HOW TO's" of Building
a Large, Successful
Direct Sales / Network Marketing
Organization

Dennis Windsor

WINDWARD
PRESS
Dallas, Texas 75374

Printed in the United States of America

Designed by David L. Showalter

ISBN: 0-9626-7910-0
LCCC# 90-50352

Permission to teach classes based upon this book reserved by the author. For information regarding classes/ training videos based upon this book, see page 254 or contact:

Windsor International
P.O. Box 850201
Richardson, TX 75085
(214) 644-7500

First printing, July 1990
Second printing, August 1990

ACKNOWLEDGEMENTS

There are many to whom I owe a deep debt of gratitude, beginning with my wife, Jill; who not only sacrificed many hours of "our" time in my writing this book, but played a major role in the editing of the manuscripts as well. Her commitment to support what I do and to help me keep balanced in life has been my greatest source of encouragement and challenge.

My assistants, Robyn Shearin and Brenda Lewis, carried extra workloads with the typing of the manuscripts, obtaining reprint permissions, research, copying thousands of pages, and assisting with the revisions of multiple manuscripts. My associate, Garry Schoen, helped in research, idea generating and the editing of the manuscripts.

Dillon Gage, a Dallas based investment firm, gave us access to the currencies and precious metals on the cover. Special thanks to Terence Hanlon, Sid Reichenberger and Gabriel Castillo III.

And last but not least, I owe a firm debt of gratitude to the Independent Distributors whom I've had the privilege to work with, learn from, help succeed and reach goals together in this great business vehicle called Direct Sales/Network Marketing. They have proven that the principles and applications of this book work!

CONTENTS

SECTION III
PROFESSIONAL TRAINING APPLICATIONS

SECTION IV
SAMPLE WORKSHEETS

FINANCIALLY FREE!

PREFACE

Have you ever dreamed of being able to take a month long vacation, and not only get paid for it, but actually see your income increase? Would building a business that wouldn't fall apart if you didn't show up for two or three weeks be appealing to you? How would you like to have the freedom to spend extra time with your family, or to be more involved with ministry or social causes, and still have your personal financial needs met, whatever they may be?

People readily admit that they would pay just about any price if they could just be "financially free". A recent *USA Today* readers' poll on "Your Money and Your Life" found that 46% of those surveyed would work 12 hours a day, six days a week, 50 weeks a year for a salary of $500,000. That kind of annual income does sound fantastic! The only problem is, if you are working that many hours, other aspects of your life such as your marriage, your children, and your hobbies would have to be neglected. Perhaps that's the reason why 42% of the readers polled would decline a position that required such long hours, even if they were offered that sort of salary. In today's society, people seem to want both money and flexibility of their time. So what is the ideal situation?

If you have the money ($50,000 - $500,000), you might consider buying a successful franchise. Or you might want to consider starting your own firm. Many people have already proven that it's possible to amass a fortune in retailing, manufacturing, or marketing. The fact is, there are dozens upon dozens of financial vehicles which can provide you with the opportunity to earn a good living in today's business marketplace. The only problem is, it's hard to find one in which your time is not in continual demand.

One of the few exceptions to this rule is a business vehicle which is commonly referred to as "Direct Sales" or "Network Marketing". These terms are used to describe an industry in which products and services are moved directly from the manufacturer to the consumer, via a network of independent contractors (who are usually referred to as distributors).

What sets the direct sales / network marketing industry apart from most traditional jobs or business ventures is the fact that people not only have the opportunity to earn a solid living on the retail sales of their products or services, but they also have the opportunity to develop other distributors for the manufacturer, and to earn "overrides" or "management bonuses" based upon these new distributors' sales volume.

Think about that! Hundreds of thousands of American professionals long for the freedom and the personal satisfaction which go hand-in-hand with owning a business of their own. But yet, most of these people either don't know how, or are reluctant to make the transition. As a network marketing distributor, you can help these people accomplish their dream of operating a lucrative business of their own, and by doing so, **you can earn an exciting income for yourself!**

John D. Rockefeller said that "I would rather earn one percent off 100 people's efforts than 100 percent off my own efforts". It's this principle which is the foundation of the direct sales or network marketing industry. In this type of business, you have the opportunity to set up an unlimited number of other distributors, either in your own geographic area or nationally, and for doing so, **the company you represent will pay you overrides or management bonuses!**

Most importantly, direct marketing companies don't just pay you on the sales of your personally recruited distributors. Instead, they pay you on several levels or generations of distributors. This means that if you develop a distributor in Chicago, who develops a distributor in Orlando, who develops a distributor in Dallas, you have the opportunity to earn commissions and bonuses based upon all of these distributors' sales volume. That's right; even though you had no previous contact with anyone but the distributor in Chicago, you can be earning bonuses and overrides off the sales activity which is taking place in all these different cities!

It's also important to note that network marketing organizations tend to grow geometrically. In other words, since each distributor that you develop will most likely develop multiple distributors, **a few key personally recruited network marketing distributors can often times result in an organization of several hundred (or several thousand) distributors.** For example, simple arithmetic will show that if you did nothing more than develop one new distributor per month, and if you taught the distributors that you developed to do the exact same thing, by the end of one year, you would have 4,095 distributors in your organization (see details in introduction). Think about that! Over 4,000 distributors would be generating product volume, and you could be earning bonuses and overrides off of every single sale! As you can imagine, the income potential can be staggering!

Best of all, **it doesn't just work "in theory"**! I personally believed that if I could take the concept of network marketing, combine it with a legitimate product or service and a lot of hard work, I would have the potential to work my way to a very substantial income. I put it to the test with two different direct marketing companies. In my first, I developed a network of over 15,000 distributors and earned over $98,000 in the first nine months. My second proved to be even more lucrative with over 30,000 distributors and earnings of over $1,000,000 during my first three years. The industry does work - I've experienced it first hand!

Obviously, earning these sort of financial rewards has been exciting. But equally important has been the freedom which this industry has allowed me! I've worked for myself, set my own hours, and traveled when and where I wanted to. I've also been able to spend extended quality time with my wife, and I've been free to commit myself to ministry and social causes. In fact, I had the pleasure of being able to take a 45 day honeymoon, and at the same time, **I had the thrill of coming back to a monthly commission check which was over $5,000 higher than my previous month's pay!**

Why me? It's not because I'm some superstar. Instead, the reason why I've been successful is partly because I work intensely hard during the hours which I devote to the business. But more importantly, the reason I've been so successful is because this exciting industry has allowed me to duplicate my efforts.

This brings me to the reason why I have written this book: to teach others the "how to's" of building a successful direct sales / network marketing organization both massively and rapidly. I hope that these key points will help you to bring to fruition your desires of being "Financially Free!"

I wish you the best of success,

Dennis Windsor

INTRODUCTION TO DIRECT SALES / NETWORK MARKETING

Welcome to one of the most exciting and profitable businesses in existence today! Direct Sales / Network Marketing (referred to as DS/NM from here on) is among the fastest growing industries worldwide and avails the opportunity to earn a serious full time income or a solid part time income. These next few pages will give you a general overview of how the industry functions, examples of its geometric growth potential, national expansion, and a few reasons why it is the optimum business opportunity.

FINANCIALLY FREE! - Being in the position of having your financial needs met, whether it's $30,000 or $300,000 a year. Able to receive this income whether you work this week or not. Therefore, it's being able to have financial income and freedom of time simultaneously.

How the Industry Functions

This system of marketing products and services is basically the same as most other businesses or industries. You have a company that manufactures a product. This company then ships the product to a location, from which it is either retailed to a consumer, or sold at wholesale to another company. The main difference between a traditional marketing company and a DS/NM company is where the majority of the revenue goes.

A traditional company's major expenses would be advertising, promotion, new market development, regional warehousing, satellite offices, middlemen commissions, etc. In DS/NM, most of the above mentioned expenses are eliminated, and therefore, more commissions are available for the distributors. In other words, you still have the same basic system of manufacturer - distributor - retail sales; you just have more dollars going to the people who actually market the product to the retail consumer(See below).

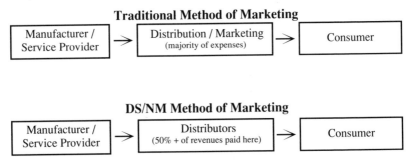

Traditional Method of Marketing

| Manufacturer / Service Provider | → | Distribution / Marketing (majority of expenses) | → | Consumer |

DS/NM Method of Marketing

| Manufacturer / Service Provider | → | Distributors (50% + of revenues paid here) | → | Consumer |

Geometric Growth Potential

Because you have higher percentages being paid directly to distributors, the opportunity exists for a large number of people to make a solid income. In fact, this greater distribution of profits is what fuels the most exciting part of the DS/NM industry - building a large, successful distributor organization.

In the forward, I mentioned that if you recruit one new distributor a month who does the same thing, by the end of one year, you would have over 4,095 distributors in your organization. Here's how that works:

Month	New Distributors	Total in Your Group
1	1	1
2	1+1+1	3
3	1+3+3	7
4	1+7+7	15
5	1+15+15	31
6	1+31+31	63
7	1+63+63	127
8	1+127+127	255
9	1+255+255	511
10	1+511+511	1023
11	1+1023+1023	2047
12	1+2047+2047	4095

These numbers are realistic and attainable with recruiting only one person a month. Think what would happen if you and your group recruited two, three, five, or ten a month? Because of the geometric growth potential, the incomes can be staggering!

National Expansion

In a traditional company, it takes a lot of time and expenses to expand nationally or internationally. This is not the case with DS/NM. You can easily develop distributors in other cities, states, or even countries. In fact, it happens as a natural part of the business building process.

For example:
You may develop a new distributor in Dallas -
Who develops a new distributor in Denver -
Who develops a new distributor in Chicago -
Who develops a new distributor in Toronto -
Who develops a new distributor in London.

In this example, your income potential is based upon the combined sales volume of what is happening in all five different cities. That's right, **even though you only personally enrolled the distributor in Dallas, you are paid on all these distributors' volume.**

Keep in mind, this illustration is with just five distributors' efforts.

When you add in the "geometric growth" potential of the DS/NM industry, the potential for national and international expansion can be unlimited!

"A DS/NM sales force is self-replicating, self-motivated and self-financed. The more distributors you recruit for your organization, the more they recruit in return; the better your people sell, the more commissions filter up to you."
- Success Magazine, May 1990

The Optimum Business Opportunity

Your diversification into this lucrative industry will prove to be one of the best business decisions you'll ever make. Whether you are seeking a supplemental income of $500 - $2,000 per month, a full time income of $3,000 - $10,000 a month, or a serious income level of $15,000+ per month, there are no other business opportunities today that can match what the the DS/NM industry offers you. Let me summarize why it is the optimum business opportunity:

1. Minimal capital required for start-up
2. No employees
3. Limited paperwork (company computer usually handles sales volume and commission due)
4. Low overhead (most distributors will work out of offices in their home.)
5. Immediate and unlimited income potential
6. Flexible schedule
7. No territorial restrictions
8. Self employed tax benefits
9. Independence - no boss!
10. A much more exciting and challenging career!

Understanding how strong this industry is and what it offers you will provide the motivation you'll need to be successful in it. Now that you've captured the potential, what you need now are the "how to's" of becoming financially free through the DS/NM industry.

As you read the next four sections, make sure you answer the questions and complete the worksheets (make photocopies of the worksheets, keeping the book as the "master"). Use this book as a continued resource to help you reach your financial objectives. By mastering the principles and applications, you'll be well on your way to becoming "Financially Free!"

"Experts predict that in the '90s, 'network marketing' will fuse Americans from coast to coast into one gigantic, pulsating sales amoeba."
    - Success Magazine, May 1990

SECTION
I

STEPS
TO
BECOMING
FINANCIALLY
FREE!

"People who have attained things worth having in this world have worked while others have idled, have persevered when others gave up in despair, and have practiced early in life the valuable habits of self-denial, industry, and singleness of purpose. As a result, they enjoy in later life the success so often erroneously attributed to good luck."

- Grenville Kleiser

CHAPTER ONE

PAY THE PRICE

If one of your desires in life is to become financially independent, and if network marketing is the financial vehicle which you have chosen to accomplish this objective, it is foundational that you be willing to "pay the price" necessary to accomplish your goals.

> *"The average person puts only 25% of his energy and ability into his work. The world takes off its hat to those who put in more than 50% of their capacity, and stands on its head for those few and far between souls who devote 100%."*
> *-Andrew Carnegie*

What do I mean by "pay the price"? Simply put, you must be willing to make the sacrifices in your life which are necessary in order for you to reach your goals. In other words, if you want to be successful, you will probably have to give up some of your free time. Specifically, in order to make time for your business, you may have to give up your Saturday golf games, watching football on the weekends, your vacation this summer, or your social time on Friday and Saturday nights.

Most People Want the Rewards, But...

Granted, those are some very significant sacrifices, and quite frankly, most people are simply not willing to make them. Instead, most people would rather take a "enjoy it while you can" or a "stop and smell the roses" type of approach to their daily lives. That's why most everyone will tell you that they want the rewards which come with being financially free. However, when it comes right down to it, a relatively small percentage actually achieve such a goal. My point being, the willingness to make such sacrifices is critical to your success in this industry.

The fact is, **anything that is worth having takes some kind of sacrifice to attain, and the greater that "anything" is, the greater the sacrifice whichmust be made.**

Doing What Others Won't

Along with having a willingness to make the necessary sacrifices, the second key aspect of "paying the price" is developing the proper attitude: an attitude that says, **"I'm going to do the kind of things that most people aren't willing to do."** I am convinced that the DS/NM industry is one of the last frontiers in which the average business person has a shot at becoming financially free. And if you are willing to go out and do the sort of things that the average network marketing distributor is not willing to do, you are a major step ahead of your competition. Therefore, if you'll make the sacrifices, and do the other things that successful people in this industry have done, you'll be well on your way to enjoying the exciting benefits that accompany success.

Singleness of Purpose

The third principle of "paying the price" is one of focus or "singleness of purpose". In other words, the time that you are spending building your organization of distributors must be completely free of any distractions or diversity towards other projects. Specifically, if you have set aside a certain number of hours per week for building your DS/NM organization, it's essential that during this time, 100% of your energies, thoughts and actions are being directed towards this one goal and this one goal only!

The fact is, since your success in this industry will be in direct proportion to your having singleness of purpose, you simply cannot expect to reach your goals if you have three or four projects that you are involved in during this time. You must be single minded!

Developing Your Vision

Your fourth principle in "paying the price" is that you have "a vision". Your vision will be different than (and should not be confused with) your goals. Your vision is an **overall picture** of where you are going, why you are doing what you are doing, and where you want to end up. Ultimately, it's your vision that will determine your level of financial freedom.

In developing your vision, the first thing that you must realize is that the company that you are representing is one thing, and one thing only. It's the financial vehicle that will take you from where you presently are (point A) to where you want to be (point B).

Point A will be different things for different people. For some, it may be being in debt, for others, it may be dissatisfaction with their current profession or discontent with their level of income. Point B would hopefully be the answer to those dilemmas. For example, it may be being debt free with a substantial savings account, job satisfaction, or being able to meet your financial needs, goals and desires.

POINT A	POINT B
In debt	Debt free with financial reserves
Job dissatisfaction	Excited about job
No free time	Freedom to come and go

Regardless of what Point A is in your life, and regardless of what you want Point B to be, it's essential that you have a grasp of where you currently are and where you want your vehicle to take you. Thus, it would be advisable for you to take a few moments, and complete your own A - B chart.

POINT A	POINT B
_____	_____
_____	_____

Why? What? How?

Once you have Points A and B firmly established, you will then need to ask yourself why you are doing what you're doing. In other words, you need to have a clear understanding of why you are sacrificing things like golfing with your friends, watching football, and your social time. Answers to these questions will stabilize your vision. When you are tired and want to rest, they will give you the needed motivation to keep going. And when others ask you (or you ask yourself), "Why are you working so hard?", you'll know the answer, and you'll have conviction!

"Decide what you want, decide what you are willing to exchange for it, establish your priorities, and go for it."

- H.L. Hunt

Finally, when developing your vision, you need to have a mental picture of where you want to end up. In other words, you need to know what you want to do once you get to Point B. Questions which will help establish this mental picture are: "What is my purpose in life?"; "How would I use the extra time I had if I were financially free?"; "What kind of positive impact do I want to have on others?" and "Once I am in this position, what will I do?".

Once you have established a mental image of your vision, it's critical that you put this image in print. In fact, in order to get the maximum benefit from this book, you should take out a notepad or your Daytimer and start working on writing down your vision before you proceed to the next chapter (see sample on next page).

When doing so, keep in mind that this explosive industry has virtually no limits, and that your vision is limited only by your dreams and imagination. In fact, since there are usually no territories or limitations in DS/NM programs, and since most companies have products or services that have a very broad consumer base, you can literally accomplish just about any financial objective you set your mind to!

Sample Vision Worksheet
(Blank copy on p. 223)
"My Vision"

My overall desire in life is: to live my life to it's maximum potential, to build a business that gives me financial freedom, and to help others reach their goals and potential also.

My top three goals for my family are:
#1. To develop a strong unity among us.
#2. To spend both quantity and quality time together.
#3. To reach out to others as a family.

My top three financial goals are:
#1. To be debt free.
#2. To earn $100,000 a year.
#3. To have a $50,000 savings account.

My top three social goals are:
#1. To build close relationships with 2 - 3 couples.
#2. To open our house to the neighborhood.
#3. To take a weekend getaway with friends.

My top three ministry / charity goals are:
#1. To devote extra time to my church.
#2. To develop a ministry to the underprivileged.
#3. To donate extra time to community projects.

My top three individual goals are:
#1. To reach the top position in my company this year.
#2. To travel to Europe next year.
#3. To set a new company monthly sales record.

When I get to be financially free, I want to: pay off all debts, fund my future income needs and divide my time between family, business and helping others to realize their dreams too!

Remember...

- Anything worth having takes some kind of sacrifice to obtain, and the greater the "anything" is, the greater the sacrifices that must be paid.

- Successful people do the things that most people aren't willing to do.

- Your success will be in direct proportion to having "singleness of purpose".

- It's important to write down your vision.

Questions to Answer

For me to be successful in this industry, a price will have to be paid. Am I willing to pay this price? Yes_____ No_____ Today's date_____

In what three specific areas am I willing to make sacrifices?

1._____

2._____

3._____

Singleness of purpose will play a key role in my road to financial freedom. What things or areas do I need to set aside right now so I can be totally focused? (i.e unprofitable businesses, current part-time businesses, etc.)

1._____

2._____

3._____

CHAPTER TWO

FOR A PERIOD OF TIME

I proposed marriage to my beautiful wife, Jill, on July 13, 1988. Much to my surprise, she knew it was coming. But not to be outwitted, I had a second proposal planned - that we get married in ten days on July 23. Nervous, but excited, we were married on that date, then honeymooned in Hawaii, the Grand Canyon, and Dallas through August 28.

Even though I took off work for 45 days, our commission check for this period went up over $5,000! This is not to brag on us, it is to demonstrate the potential of this great industry.

Why was I able to take this time off and still see my income rise? It was because I was willing to "pay the price". That's right, I had no problem committing to making the sacrifices it took to get where I wanted to be, because I knew that this price only had to be paid **"for a period of time"**.

Most people are driven to work hard all of their lives with the hope of one day retiring. This industry offers more than that. If offers the potential to build an income base that requires less time and energy the longer that you are involved. This means that you don't have to wait for retirement to take time off, vacation, travel or spend time with your family. The DS/NM industry gives you the opportunity to enjoy these rewards throughout your career.

How long?

How long must a person be willing to "pay the price"? A rule of thumb would be that you commit to a minimum time period of six to twelve months to build a solid foundation in your business. It is during this foundational building period that the most sacrifices, the hardest work, the longest hours and the most well implemented strategy will be necessary. It is also during this period that your vision (which you have just written down) needs to be the most clearly defined and understood by yourself, your family and your key distributors. Six to twelve months is not a long time. It will go by extremely fast. The rewards will be worth it!

Obviously, six to twelve months is just a "ball park figure". In actuality, your individual financial goals will determine the amount of time you will need to invest; and the greater these goals are, the greater the amount of time required. In other words, supplemental financial goals will require part time hours and will result in part time rewards. Full time income goals will require full time efforts and will yield greater rewards. And if your desire is to become financially free through this industry, you will be called upon during this foundational building stage to devote almost all available day, evening and weekend hours. However, the rewards for doing so will be incredible! (Remember my honeymoon illustration!)

Shown below is a chart which will help you to understand the hours needed to reach different financial goals.

Monthly Financial Goal	Number of Hours Required	Length of Time
$500 - $1,000	10 - 20 weekly	6 Months
$3,000 - $5,000	40 - 50 weekly	12 Months
$8,000 - $10,000	60 - 80 weekly	12 -24 Months

To earn a supplemental income ($500 - $1,000 per month), you will need to work 10 - 20 hours weekly. Your "period of time" committed to "pay the price" should be a minimum of six months. To reach a full time income level ($3,000 - $5,000 monthly), you should work hard 40 - 50 hours a week. This typically requires a minimum foundation building period of twelve months. If your goal is to become financially free, you will need to commit to 60 - 80 hours of intensive work weekly for a minimum time period of one to two years.

Goal Setting

When you are setting your goals, keep the following points in mind:

A) **Goals must be realistic.** It's alright to have big dreams, but don't set fantasy goals. If it takes one to two years to develop a solid six figure income base, don't set your goals at six months. Make them realistic!

B) **Goals must be measurable.** Set your goals in steps or intervals so you can track your results as you go. Be sure to set immediate goals (next six months), short term goals (one to five years), and long term goals (six to ten years).

C) **Goals must be specific.** When setting your goals, don't do so in general terms. An example of being too general would be to say "I want to own a house someday." Instead, sit down and figure out where you are financially, what income will be needed, and the realistic time needed to get there. Then, set a specific type of house, price range, down payment needed, and on which date you would like to purchase it. Be specific!

"There is no achievement without goals."
-Robert J. McKain

D) **Goals must be flexible!** This is critical to understand, If you fail to reach your goals, don't fall apart or quit. Ascertain why you didn't make it, figure out how much longer it will take, and adjust your goals. Be persistent in reaching your goals, but most of all, be flexible!

E) **Goals must be supportable!** If you are single, you have a lot of flexibility as far as time commitments and responsibilities. However, if you have a family, you probably have less flexibility and more responsibilities. Either way, it is important to stay somewhat balanced. Keep your priorities in line. If you are going to make sacrifices that will affect others (especially your family), make sure that they are communicated and agreed upon in advance.

Keep in mind that paying the price won't be easy. Many times you will have the desire to slow down or even quit. What will help pull you through these times is your knowledge of the fact that you're "paying the price" only "for a period of time". Don't forget it!

At this point, take a few moments and write down some of your initial goals (See page 193 for a blank Initial Goals Worksheet).

EXAMPLE OF
MY INITIAL GOALS

	1st TWO WEEKS	1st MONTH	1st 90 DAYS	1st SIX MONTHS	1st YEAR	
APPLICATION COMPLETED	√					
AMOUNT OF INITIAL ORDER	$2500					
WHO DO YOU KNOW LIST	√					
TOP TEN SELECTED	√					
PEOPLE CONTACTED	10	15	45	90	180	
PRODUCT/ OPPORTUNITY PRESENTATIONS	10	15	45	90	180	
OPPORTUNITY MEETINGS ATTENDED WITH GUEST	4	16	48	96	192	
VIDEOS PLACED	10	15	45	90	180	
DISTRIBUTORS SPONSORED	6	10	20	40	60	
PRODUCT SOLD	$1000	$2500	$7500	$15000	$30000	
WHOLESALE VOLUME MOVED	$10000	$20000	$100000	$300000	$1000000	
TITLE REACHED	Entry	Level A	Level B	Level C	Level D	
INCOME EARNED	$750	$2000	$7500	$24000	$80000	

Remember...

• Part time efforts yield part time rewards.
• Full time efforts yield full time rewards.
• Goals must be realistic, measurable, specific, flexible, and supportable.

Action Point

1. Complete Initial Goals Worksheet.

CHAPTER THREE

VISION / VEHICLE PRINCIPLE

Vision - A vivid concept or object of imaginative contemplation. A vivid, imaginative conception or anticipation. (Websters)

Vehicle - A means of accomplishing a purpose. (Random House Dictionary)

Earlier, we established that the vision which you have for both your life and your business will have a profound effect upon the level of success which you ultimately achieve in this industry. We also noted that it is critical that you have laid out on paper where you want to go in life and what role your new business will play in meeting your objectives. If you have not yet put your vision on paper, refer back to p. 29 for an outline.

I now want to emphasize the fact that your vision will not only effect the level of success which you achieve, but it will greatly influence the overall vision of the people you bring into your organization. If you have small goals (and a limited vision), your people will most likely have small goals and a limited vision. On the other hand, if your vision is one of greatness, many of the people that you recruit will develop visions of greatness.

> *"Singleness of purpose is one of the chief essentials for success in life; no matter what may be one's aim."*
> *- John D. Rockefeller, Jr.*

Realizing that your vision has such an important bearing on the vision of your distributors, it's absolutely essential that you wholeheartedly believe that the specific Direct Sales / Network Marketing Company which you have chosen to represent is THE business vehicle that can allow you to reach your financial goals. If you believe this, so will your distributors. On the other hand, if you have doubts, so will the people who you have recruited. And anytime that you or anyone else has lingering doubts about the viability of the company which is being represented, it becomes very difficult to "pay the price" which is necessary for success. For this reason, after you have carefully chosen the company you will represent, demonstrate confidence that it is a phenomenal business opportunity!

A Sense of Urgency

I once saw the quote, "When life gives you a wave, ride it to the end." Building your organization is somewhat like that. As you are creating momentum, maximize its potential, and get ready to create more. Don't be satisfied with the first wave (or with one new distributor). Keep pressing to catch the next one (creating new sales). This is basically known as having a "sense of urgency" in your work ethics. **The timing is now, not tomorrow. Business is plentiful now; capture as much of the market as you can.**

"The speed of the leader determines the rate of the pack."   *- Anonymous*

In Chapter one, you learned that anything in life worth having takes sacrifice; and the greater that anything is, the greater the sacrifices which must be made. Since you now have an "open window" to a lot of new business, take your time off later. Demonstrate "by example" to your distributors that it is important to "strike the iron while it's hot"!

Getting Others to Commit Full Time

One of the keys to building a large, successful organization is being able to successfully impart your vision to others. In fact, if you can get a group of people caught up in the vision that they too can earn a highly sig-

"The leader seeks to communicate his vision to his followers. He captures their attention with his optimistic intuition of possible solutions to their needs. He influences them by the dynamism of his faith. He demonstrates confidence that the challenge can be met, the need resolved, the crisis overcome."

- John Haggai
Lead on!

nificant income with your company, they will be much more apt to become highly committed, full time distributors. Thus, when building your organization, present your opportunity in a manner that challenges them to make that type of commitment. Reinforce this challenge by introducing them to others who have achieved great things working full time!

If you can develop the "right vision" (one that projects an aura of greatness, and one that projects with absolute certainty that your company is the vehicle which can allow a person to meet their financial objectives), and if you can get enough people caught up in this vision, you will reach your financial goals almost automatically.

Let me refer back to my definition of being financially free. It's having your income needs met (no matter how large or small) and having freedom of time. This is where it is critical to get others caught up in the vision-vehicle commitment. In this industry you will have the opportunity to earn management bonuses on your organization's sales volume. Most times, however, you must meet certain performance requirements in order to receive these commissions. Therefore, the more people you have caught up in the vision - vehicle commitment, the more often you will meet your management bonus override requirements through these people's efforts alone. This, in turn, will create the financial freedom you are working so hard for.

Remember...

- You must firmly believe that your chosen company is the vehicle to fulfill your vision.

- Your success in this industry will be greatly determined by your ability to impart or communicate your vision to others.

CHAPTER FOUR

MANAGING YOUR TIME

Time management is an extremely important factor in building a successful Direct Sales / Network Marketing organization. For this reason, you need to keep things in proper perspective, and you need to have a game plan as to where to best spend your time and efforts.

In order to develop such a game plan, let's take a moment and refer back to a couple of key points which have previously been established. First of all, we've already established the fact that in order to be successful in this industry, you need to have a high number of people in your organization **who are committed to your company** and who are making a great living from it. Secondly, we've already established **that most of the people that you recruit won't be willing to pay the price that it takes to be successful in this industry.** Realizing these two points, you need to understand that building a successful direct marketing organization is basically "a numbers game" (especially at first). That's right, it's a numbers game, and you will probably need to recruit and train as many as 25 to 75 personally sponsored distributors in order to have 5 to 15 key leaders surface.

80% - 20% Rule

In order to maximize your profits, you will want to spend the majority of your time developing new personally sponsored and downline distributors. In fact, based upon the guidelines of the *USA Today* study on the following page, you should spend close to eighty percent of your time in the development side of your business. This means that you should spend close to eighty percent of your time recruiting new distributors, training them to be effective, and generating new leads and/or contacts throughout your organization.

Where Salespeople Spend Their Time

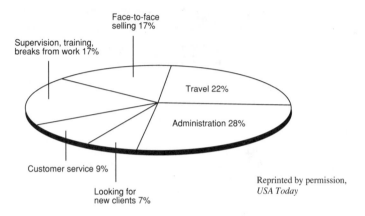

Face-to-face selling 17%

Supervision, training, breaks from work 17%

Travel 22%

Administration 28%

Customer service 9%

Looking for new clients 7%

Reprinted by permission, *USA Today*

Building Your Organization

Recruiting new distributors - During your initial six to twelve months, recruiting will be the lifeblood of your business, and you should focus on bringing into your business just as many new distributors as you feel that you can comfortably work with. For most people, this number ranges from 25 to 75 people. When you are prospecting, keep in mind that there is no room for falsehoods such as, "I can't think of anyone who would be interested in a serious business opportunity." The fact is, there are always potential distributors no matter what your chosen field. It simply takes hustle to locate and develop them.

Train them to be effective - Once someone has made the commitment that your company will be their financial vehicle, you should spend solid time training them. First of all, teach them the details of your company's product line or service, and make sure that they use the products religiously. Secondly, educate them on how the business / compensation plan works, and what sort of earnings are possible. Thirdly, give them all of the written information you have on the industry which your company is a part of. Finally, help them put together a list of potential prospects, and then help them schedule several business opportunity presentations on which you can accompany them.

Developing new leads and/or contacts - People everywhere (whether they are well off financially, or struggling to make ends meet) are looking for an opportunity. As a result, there are hundreds of thousands of potential new distributors for your company. Listed below are some examples of different areas where you can look to generate leads.(See recruiting scripts on p. 111 for ideas on how to contact these prospects.)

Personal Contacts
Who do you know list (See p. 197)

Referrals
Constantly ask "Do you know someone who might be interested?"

Advertising
Local newspapers
National newspapers
Business Magazines (*Inc.*, *Fortune*, *Entrepreneur*, etc.)
Radio and TV
Direct mail
Personnel services
Yellow Pages
TV Guide or local TV schedules
Military base newspapers
College, University newspapers
Help wanted / Jobs available bulletin boards at
Universities / Churches

Cold Call Research
Listings in Yellow pages
Service listings in newspapers
Newspaper advertisers (reverse their ad - tell them about your company)
Newspaper profiles of successful business people (realtor or insurance agent of the month, etc.)

Trade Shows
Check with a city's Chamber of Commerce for a list of upcoming shows.

Retail Your Product

If you are spending eighty percent of your time in the development side of your business, the remaining twenty percent should be spent selling your company's product. When doing so, be sure to keep good records so that when your company comes out with a new product or service, you can go back to your current customer base. Also keep in mind that many of your retail customers will like your company's products so much, they will end up wanting to become distributors. How many retail customers is it possible to develop? **Retail selling is much like recruiting: If you are willing to hustle, you will never run out of new customers!**

The 80% - 20% rule is primarily applicable to distributors who are looking to build a large organization and to provide themselves with a means of achieving true financial independence. If such a goal is not your primary goal, and if your main purpose of enrolling in your company is to earn some extra cash quickly, you should reverse the rule. In other words, you should spend eighty percent of your time retailing (so you can earn commissions quickly), and you can devote the remaining twenty percent to building an organization.

"So long as new ideas are created, sales will continue to reach new highs."
- Charles F. Ketering

Maximizing Your Time

Once you have made the commitment to "pay the price" that it will take to be successful, it's important that you make the most of the time you have available to you! This is especially important during the formative stages of building your organization.

For example, if you experience some success (i.e. recruiting a new distributor or making a big retail sale), don't be tempted to spend the rest of the day sitting by the pool. Such actions can cause you to lose valuable time and momentum, and they set the wrong example for your organization. There will be plenty of time for relaxing after you have your organization

Energy + momentum = Enthusiasm

built, so while you are still in the active building stages, make every available minute count!

Daily Activity Suggestions

Whether you are full time or part time, there will be occasions when you do not have appointments scheduled. During such time periods, there are a number of productive activities that can help you to reach your goals more quickly.

Phone Calls - You can do at least half of your business in this industry over the phone. Therefore, always keep your list of "top distributors", and your "who do you know" list with you. And when you have free moment between or after meetings, put the time to use by touching base with your new recruits and distributors. Let them know that things are really taking off. Pass something new and exciting on to them (maybe a new sales technique, or type of person to recruit). You can also use this time to contact someone new on your "who do you know" list. Use the phone, use the phone, use the phone!

Strategy sessions - Whether you are by yourself, or with a group of distributors, fill free time thinking about how to expand your business. Here are a few things to strategize about:

- new market areas
- ads that work
- role playing
- discussing successful experiences
- questions and answers
- upcoming events and meetings
- setting new appointments
- training
- reviewing goals
- updating your "who do you know" list

. termindogy

Read, listen, watch! - There is a tremendous amount of material available to expand your skills and knowledge of the industry. You should spend at least one or two hours a week reading books, publications, or research information, listening to teaching and motivational cassettes, and watching videos that teach you new skills or exciting things about your company.

Take the meeting to someone - You will **never** run out of new leads in your business if you are willing to hustle. There is no such thing as saturation of your products or opportunity. Find someone new today that has never heard of your opportunity, and take the product / video to them. Constantly be meeting with people!

You are in the sales/marketing/distributor development business. Spend your time calling your people, selling your products, attending meetings, and teaching your people to do the same. By maximizing your time, you will be on the fastest track towards building a large, successful organization, and enjoying the freedom and lifestyle which this industry offers.

Remember...

• Spend 80% of your time building, 20% retailing.

• Don't let up when you experience success.

Action Points

1. Select several new methods from the preceding lists to develop new leads / contacts.

A. _____

B._____

C._____

2. Develop a retail record keeping system.

   • 3 1/2 X 5 file cards filed by month sold
     - include name and products bought.
     - follow up with new products released.

   • Retail log (8 1/2 X 11)
     - monthly sales or
     - product sales

Know your weekly PV out-the-door.

CHAPTER FIVE

RECRUIT UP!

BIG-COMPANY EXODUS
Fired managers start their own companies

Nearly half a million corporate executives, administrators, and managers lost their jobs between 1981 and 1985, the latest years for which the Bureau of Labor Statistics has figures. Since then that number can only have grown, given the spate of corporate mergers and acquisitions and the continued downsizing by large companies.

What's surprising, though, is how many of these former pinstripers have decided to launch their own enterprises.

Currently, reports one Chicago outplacement firm, 17% of the displaced executives it sees are starting their own businesses instead of returning to corporate life. Three years ago, according to Challenger, Gray & Christmas Inc. (CGC), the rate was 7%.

Interest in start-ups is particularly high among senior execs, those who formerly earned six-figure incomes, and among professional and technical specialists. About 20% of laid-off execs are choosing jobs at small companies, often in exchange for equity, says Drake Beam Morin Inc., a New York outplacement firm.

The backgrounds of the people running INC. 100 public companies tend to confirm the trend. In the class of 1983, 49% of INC. 100 CEO's reported having previous big-business experience. Five years later, about two-thirds of the responding CEO's among the 1988 INC. 100 companies said they had come out of the big-business world.

Many corporate emigres are seeking financial security foremost, according to CGC president James E. Challenger; indeed, they originally took positions in large corporations because they thought those jobs offered security. Having been laid off, they are turning to <u>entrepreneurship</u> to become their own bosses and regain the <u>security</u> they once had. As a result, says Challenger, "They tend to take less risk. Their [start-ups] tend to be well thought out.   *-Amy Schulman*

One of the keys to rapidly building a large organization (one that explodes across the country) is having the ability to recruit high caliber people - people who have talent, skills, know-how, contacts, and a burning desire to succeed. You should look for people who are either already "at the top", or people who have previously been "at the top", but for one reason or another, have had some setbacks.

The Entrepreneur Explosion

Where do you find such people? As Ms. Shulman of *Inc.* magazine wrote in the above article, nearly half a million talented people lost their jobs between 1981 and 1985. (Our research indicates that at least another half million were laid off between 1985 and 1989.) The article also indicates that of those who were laid off, over 17% started their own businesses.

This indicates that tens of thousands of key people are looking to create their own financial security rather than depend upon other companies to provide it for them. These people want to be paid what they think they are worth. They want both the challenge of being an entrepreneur and the freedom that comes with owning one's own business! What these people are looking for is simply the right financial vehicle. This is where your opportunity to recruit serious minded, high caliber professionals comes in. They are looking for the "right business" to get into, and all that you need to do is present your opportunity to them in the proper manner and to convince them that your company is the vehicle that will allow them to reach their professional and financial goals.

Granted, in the past, it may have been difficult to attract such people. But this is not so today! The direct marketing industry currently enjoys a much more solid image than it has in years gone by, and high caliber people are very open to the incredible opportunities which our industry offers.

Be Willing to "Lay it On the Line"

At times, it can be intimidating to approach high caliber people with an opportunity. It also can be difficult for professionals to approach their peer group with a business venture (i.e. lawyer-lawyer, banker-banker,etc.) Once you're committed to a company though, it will be essential that you have enough confidence in it that you'll be willing to contact other leaders as well.

Sure it is a risk to approach these people. Risk of rejection, social status, etc. are some of the fears of professionals. However, **if your business has incredible potential and you know it, it's worth the risk!** Listen to what the Space Shuttle Challenger crew's family members wrote to the American public after the tragic accident in which the entire crew died. They wrote **"If they were alive and could speak to all Americans, we believe the Challenger crew would say this: Do not fear risk. All exploration, all growth is a calculated risk. ...without challenge, people cannot reach their highest selves. Only if we can accept our problems as challenges can today's dreams become tomorrow's realities. Only if we are willing to walk over the edge can we become winners!"**

"I do not fear failure. I only fear the 'slowing up' of the engine inside of me which is pounding, saying, 'keep going, someone must be on top, why not you?'"

- George S. Patton

Leaders today are looking for the kind of vehicle you're offering them in the DS/NM business. Walk over the edge of your hesitations and recruit them!

The Right Ingredients

This is not to say that such people are easily recruited. The fact is, most of these key leaders are very cautious about what company they will associate themselves with. But if you can present them with the "right company" in the right manner, the possibilities are limitless.

Following is a list of some of the key ingredients that most professionals are looking for in a business opportunity.

1. **Timing** - Most successful companies will experience rapid growth (500 - 1,000 percent a year) during their formative years (5 - 10). The growth rate may then begin leveling off at around 10% to 20% a year. Typically, **the financial rewards are greater if you are representing a company that is either in its growth stage or one that has products coming out that are new and explosive.** As a result, most pro's will insist upon being associated with such a company.

2. **Stability** - Entrepreneurs like start-up operations, but they really don't like bouncing from one thing to another every eight or ten months. Instead, most are looking for an opportunity with a financially stable company that has less of a risk factor than what is typically associated with a "shoe string" type operation.

3. **Management** - It is important to demonstrate to your potential new distributors that your company is run by capable professionals. Specifically, your corporate president, and the top management team need to know how to run a growing company. This is critical for high caliber people who are looking for the right business opportunity.

4. **Product** - In terms of product, professional people usually prefer to be associated with a "recognized need" type of product. They like to deal with products which have a high consumer awareness level as opposed to those in which they have to convince consumers that they need. A product needs to have some sort of "timing" to it.

Why Leaders Are Looking

The *Inc*. Magazine article reveals the high number of professionals who are looking for their own business. They are in this search usually for a wide variety of reasons. It is important to know not only what they are looking for, but why they are looking for a business they can call their own. Listed below are a few identifiable reasons why serious minded pro's are searching for a different business vehicle.

1. **Change of Career** - Many people are burned out on trying to climb

the corporate ladder. Show them how they can take their work skills and ethics, apply them to your opportunity, and become highly successful in it.

2. **Change of Industry** - There are numerous industries whose timing has come and gone, leaving talented people in the wake without jobs. Examples include real estate, construction, investment brokers, etc. Show these people that all they need is a product or company in which the "timing" is right.

3. **Laid off / Fired from Job** - If you can find someone who is in such a position, show them how your opportunity can meet their financial needs immediately.

4. **Dissatisfied with current income level** - These people want a little more out of life and are willing to work for it. Show them how much your opportunity can mean to them in terms of increased income.

5. **Dreamed of owning their own company all of their life** - These people have been looking for an ideal business opportunity that they can pour their heart into, and which can provide them with the sort of income they feel that they are worth. Show them how and why direct marketing really is the perfect business.

The important thing to remember in recruiting is that all you have to do is show your potential distributor that your opportunity can help them reach their financial goals faster. If they believe it will, they will pour their efforts into it!

Be Persistent!

Many times, when contacting leaders, you'll hear that they're "tied up" or "maxed out" right now with what they're currently doing. They may also say that they're not interested at this point in what you're offering. The important thing is to not take this as a firm "no". Respond with, "Sally, there's no pressure from me. I'll keep you posted as things progress." This leaves the door open to relay your success stories back to them.

Harvey Mackay, president of Mackay Envelopes, Inc. and author of "*Swim with the Sharks Without Being Eaten Alive*", tells the story of how it took six years to get an order from one prospect. He spent the first three years calling on them without ever being asked to quote a job. The fourth year he was asked to bid on one, but it was two more before he got an order! That is persistence!

"It's the constant and determined effort that breaks down all resistance, sweeps away all obstacles."
- Claude M. Bristol

Winston Churchill, speaking to his high school alma mater, told this group of future adults to "Never give up! Never give up! Never give up! Never, never, never, never, never give up!" This is sound advice, especially if the person you're trying to recruit has serious potential.

Successful Leadership

Dr. John Haggai, founder and director of the world renowned Haggai Institute for Advanced Leadership, has written extensively on the subject of leaders. His definition of leadership is "The discipline of deliberately exerting special influence within a group to move it toward goals of beneficial permanence that fulfill the groups real need."

Listed below are some of the traits that have characterized people who've been successful in DS/NM:

Traits of a Leader
Leaders possess a positive attitude.
Leaders are enthusiastic.
Leaders are problem solvers, not problem makers.
Leaders are self disciplined.
Leaders set the example in work habits / dedication.
Leaders dress professionally.
Leaders are risk takers.
Leaders are servants.

Do not hesitate to introduce your opportunity to high caliber people. Simply put yourself in these people's shoes, understand why they are looking to get into business for themselves, and tailor your presentation of the direct marketing industry (and your company) to these specific needs. If you will do so, you will find that recruiting high caliber people is extremely rewarding, and you will see your organization grow at an astounding rate of speed.

Remember...

• Recruit the highest caliber, most serious minded professionals you can find.

• There are identifiable reasons leaders are searching for a new business opportunity. Know what they are.

Action Point

1. Write and memorize the key ingredients your company offers.

CHAPTER SIX

BUILDING NATIONALLY / INTERNATIONALLY

One of the great benefits of the Direct Sales / Network Marketing industry is that there are no exclusive territories. This means that you not only have the opportunity to develop a distributor base in your own geographic area, but you can develop one anywhere that you are willing to put forth the effort, whether it be locally, regionally, nationally, or even internationally.

Before getting into any specific details about building a national organization, I want to point out the fact that since we live in such a mobile society, and since most people have friends and relatives scattered across the country, you will eventually develop a national organization, regardless of whether or not you purposely set out to do so. However, if you want to expedite this growth, there are several steps which have been proven to be effective.

Build Your Foundation First

First of all, it's important that you develop a strong local base of distributors, either in your own metropolitan area or in cities that are within a two to three hour driving distance. Not only will this provide you with a cash flow to build nationally, it will provide you with an inexpensive proving ground to test out your ideas, to perfect your presentation skills, and to develop a personal success story before you "hit the road".

Since most towns or cities can sustain a large number of distributors, I recommend that you personally sponsor several key people, and build several different "lines" within in your own geographic area. Generally, the most effective way to accomplish this task is to conduct weekly or bi-weekly opportunity meetings and training sessions.

Expanding Out

As you are firmly establishing your local distributor base, start thinking about building nationally. When doing so, you will probably want to select two or three major metropolitan areas in which to target your efforts. (Depending upon your company's policies, these metropolitan areas might even be out of the country.) How you select these areas should be influenced by your contacts in such areas, by the demand for your product in such areas, and by the population and economy of the specific areas which you have in mind.

After you have settled upon the area or areas in which you want to concentrate your efforts, write down a list of all of the personal and business contacts that you have in that area. Make your initial contact with these people by telephone, and send preliminary information packages to the interested parties before you go into that city. In other words, try and develop some momentum before you arrive!

"Success doesn't come to you...you go to it."
- Marva Collins

Based on personal experience, I would suggest that you do not attempt to personally sponsor more than one or two of your contacts in any geographic area (outside of your local metropolitan area). It's usually better to choose one or two key people from your list of contacts, and build underneath them, than to try and personally enroll a dozen or more first level distributors. When you have found the one or two key people that you will personally enroll, your next goal should be to build stability underneath them. To do so, you will want to teach them to do the same sort of things which you did in your local area. In other words, you will want to teach them to start several different "lines" and to hold weekly opportunity and training sessions. Once you have done so, you will have a solid foundation of activity in that particular area, and you can move on to your next targeted area.

Generating National Leads

If you do not have enough personal contacts in a geographic area which you would like to develop, advertising can be a viable option. Classified advertisements can be placed in the help wanted and/or business opportunities sections on the local papers. The most efficient way to interview those who respond to your advertisements is to conduct 2 or 3 group interviews daily (10:00 AM, 2:00 PM, 7:30 PM) at a local hotel or office suite. Hotel rooms that have a parlor room attached to the bedroom (such as those at Embassy Suites) are perfect for opening up new areas because you can conduct small group meetings right in your hotel room. (See sample advertisements on p. 123.)

To give themselves a "local identity", many successful national recruiters obtain what is commonly referred to as a "voice mailbox" in the area that they are going to be building. This allows them to place local phone numbers in their classified advertisements and may increase the response rate.

Direct mail advertising is another excellent source for prospects. Before going into an area, you may wish to purchase a list of business opportunity seekers, small business owners, realtors, insurance agents (or any other segment of the population who seems to be interested in your opportunity). You can then mail these people something which is designed to arouse their curiosity, and those who respond can be met with either "one on one" or on a group basis when you are in town. (See sample direct mail solicitations on p. 129.) You can also bring in new distributors through "cold calling". Potential prospects can be found by looking through local newspapers for advertisements from local business owners who might be interested in adding your products or services to their existing line. The yellow pages are another excellent source of prospects.

"Make the iron hot by striking it."
- Oliver Cromwell

When initiating "cold calls", a sample opening might be: "Mr Smith, my name is Bob Jones from Chicago. I'm in the(Your product/

service)industry and we're diversifying into this market. We'd like to talk to you about the potential of your company being one of our key distributors locally." or "Mr. Smith, I noticed your advertisement in the newspaper. I've got a business that would blend very well with what you are doing. I'd like to get together and review it with you." (For additional scripts, see p. 111.)

How to recruit Nationally

What to say - Your initial phone call to someone in another city can make or break you. If you are calling people that you know, it is important to communicate up front that you've diversified into a new business. If you are doing cold calls, you will want to communicate that you are bringing a new product into their area. Use controlled enthusiasm, be confident, and speak briefly on your success and the market potential. Keep them curious and anxious to meet with you or to receive the information packet which you will be sending.

What to send - An information package should include a product sample, video, product brochure, marketing plan explanation, success stories, order form, application (with your name on it), and a short note encouraging them to watch the video first! Keep this package short and to the point, and if possible, send it via an overnight courier. This shows that you are serious, and helps establish a "sense of urgency".

How to follow-up - A day or two after someone has received the information package, call them and ask, "Weren't you impressed with the video?" Then communicate to them how things have really taken off in your area, and that you'd like to **help** them capture some of the local market. Share other people's success stories, and let them know how well you think they could do. If there are "local support groups", get them in contact with one. Call the local leaders for time and locations and tell them who you will be sending. If possible, get them signed up before you send them to the meeting. You never know who they might run into at the meeting (i.e. their brother-in-law might already be in the business).

Getting a commitment - Let your prospect know that you are looking for a local person to build under. Tell him/her what it takes to get started (initial product orders, etc.), communicate the sign up cost, and ask him/her to fill out the application and return it to you as quickly as possible. As soon as it's feasible, go out and work with this person.

How to Build Internationally

If you are considering crossing international borders in the recruitment of new distributors, you should follow the same basic plan which I just covered in building nationally. However, before entering its marketplace, you research the country in depth, determine who your competition is, and target the cities where you feel you will have the most success.

In addition to the lead sources mentioned in the previous section, the following agencies or organizations can be good sources for international leads.

•Your native country's Embassy in targeted country
 (contact commercial attache officers)
•Your native country's Commerce Department in targeted country
•Your native country's trade agency in targeted country
•Your native country's consulate office in targeted cities
•Your native country's trade agencies
•Your target country's trade organizations
•Your target country's local Chamber of Commerce agencies
•Your target country's sales training organizations
•Your target country's business consultants

Each of the previously mentioned techniques has worked extremely well. Since there are no financial or physical boundaries in this industry, don't hesitate to use them to take your chosen company nationally or internationally just as fast as you can!

Remember...

• Build your local base as a foundation.

• Develop national contacts as quickly as possible.

• Use overnight delivery services to communicate a "sense of urgency".

Action Point

CONTACTS ADVERTISING DIRECT MAIL COLD CALL

1. Three cities I plan to target are:

A. _____ ___ ___ ___ ___

B. _____ ___ ___ ___ ___

C. _____ ___ ___ ___ ___

CHAPTER SEVEN

MAKE IT DUPLICATABLE

T he following quote is a great concept. However, very few people are ever able to experience the reality of it. Unless you have the capital to buy a company or franchise; unless you inherit a company or position from your family; or unless you are fortunate enough to work yourself into a senior position within a company, earning a percentage of another person's efforts is virtually an impossibility! That is, unless you get involved in direct marketing!

> *"I would rather earn 1% off 100 people's efforts than 100% off my own efforts."*
> *- John D. Rockefeller*

As a direct marketing distributor, you start out as the head of your own company! That's right, you start out **at the top**, and you not only have the opportunity to develop a network of distributors, but you have the opportunity to earn a percentage of your entire group's efforts. In fact, the potential to earn a serious income through the duplication of your efforts is one of the most exciting aspects of this industry. This chapter is written to help you get a greater understanding of the importance of, and the "how to's" involved in duplicating your efforts.

The "How To's" of Duplication

When it comes to duplication, the "golden rule" is to keep everything simple! You will want to make things understandable, but don't go into much depth. You will want to make things technical, but not so technical that you lose your prospect's attention. By following such guidelines, you will accomplish your goals in a manner which is easily reproduced by a new distributor.

Following is a brief discussion of the primary areas which you will need to keep duplicatable:

The Use of the Telephone

Your initial conversation with a potential distributor will most often occur via the telephone. When you are making such calls, keep in mind that you are not only introducing them to your business, but you are establishing a pattern which they will need to follow if they decide that they are interested in your business. For this reason, even your initial telephone procedures must be kept duplicatable. Realizing this, here are a few things to keep in mind when using the telephone:

1. **Use as little small talk as possible.** In other words, get to the point quickly. Example: "Hi Bob, Steve here. How are you doing? Great! Listen, the main reason for my call is that I've found something I think you'd be interested in."

2. **Be professional.** Know your products and company. Know what you are going to say before you call. Use phrases such as:
   • "I'm involved in a new project."
   • "I've diversified into a new business."
   • "I'd like you to come to a business briefing."
   • "I've diversified into the network marketing industry."
   • "You'll be impressed."
   • "It's a very lucrative industry."

3. **Be enthusiastic!** Let your prospect know that you are excited about this opportunity or product. However, don't overwhelm them. Control your enthusiasm.

4. **Know where you want the call to lead.** Establish a purpose for your call before you dial the number. Examples of what your pur-

pose might be are: inviting your prospect to a company briefing or setting an appointment for you to come to your prospect's home or office to show him/her your products or opportunity.

5. **Be informative, but keep their curiosity up.** When conversing with your prospect, try not to come across as elusive. Instead, give him/her just enough information to arouse curiosity, and make your prospect anxious to get together with you.

6. **Don't stay on the phone too long.** Let your prospect know that you've got a lot going on and that you are having success with this new business. Example: "Great. I'll see you Tuesday at 7:00. I've got to keep moving. I've got a few more calls to make tonight. See you then!"

Retail Sales Appointments

If your company has a written retail sales plan, it's usually best to follow it. If a written plan is not available, it is best to let your products themselves do most of the selling. When embarking on a retail sales appointment, here are a few suggestions to follow:

- Let your prospect know up front that you can't stay too long. You've got other appointments to make.

- If the husband and wife will both be needed to make a buying decision, make sure they'll both be there at your initial presentation. (Whether or not this is applicable depends upon the type of products you are marketing.)

- Follow your company's plan, or set up an environment to let them try your products. (If possible, let them try the product for a few days, and then return to close the sale.)

- If your company has a video, show selected parts of it. Usually a video will have good testimonials that will help sell your products.

- Set up a follow-up appointment.

* Note: After you have closed a sale, always ask for referrals. These will be your best leads for additional sales. (See p. 218 - 221 for referral charts and forms.)

Recruiting Packages

The purpose of a recruiting package is not to sponsor someone. Instead, it's purpose is to arouse someone's curiosity to the point that they will want to know more about your opportunity. Thus, a good recruiting package should be concise enough so that your prospects will be able to review it within 30 - 45 minutes, and it should be informative enough so that they will know whether or not they want additional information.

The following items should be included in a recruiting package:

1. A company brochure on the products / services you're marketing.

2. A distributor application. (Type in your name and distributor ID#)

3. A product order form.

4. A sheet giving an overview of the marketing / compensation plan.

5. Copies of your or your sponsor's commission checks. (These will substantiate the earning potential.)

6. A company video with income / product testimonials.

7. One or two copies of news media coverage on your company or its products.

8. A short, instructional note written on professional letterhead(See example).

Example:

Dear Sally,

It was great talking to you Friday! Enclosed is information on (<u>your company's name</u>).

Take a serious look, Sally. The video lasts about 15 minutes. I'll call you in the next couple of days to give you further details.

I look forward to talking to you.

Sincerely,

Linda

Again, the real key here is that your package be impressive and that it can be reviewed in 30 - 45 minutes.

Business Opportunity Meeting Format

Group meetings can be instrumental in building your organization because once you have a small base of distributors established, they can allow you to present your opportunity to multiple prospects. The reason this is so important is twofold: First of all, it allows you to spend your time more productively. Secondly, group meetings confirm to your guests that the opportunity is viable and that others are achieving success with your company.

It is important to conduct your group meetings in quality locations. Suggested locations would be:

- A successful distributor's home
- A local hotel conference room
- An office conference room
- A local civic center meeting room

Atmosphere is critical. Since many potential new distributors will be skeptical of an opportunity, it's essential that you present your opportunity well at such meetings. To make the best possible impression, be professional, show enthusiasm, and demonstrate success! Play upbeat music to keep everything on a positive note.

When you are conducting group meetings, always keep in mind that your presentation is establishing a pattern for others to follow. In other words, if the people in the audience should decide to become distributors, they should be able to give the same sort of meeting which you are giving. For this reason, it's best to keep explanations of the products and marketing plan on an "easy to understand" level. Give impressive facts and examples, but don't get too technical. Let the brochures that you will hand out at the end of your meeting give the more technical information.

Formal opportunity meetings should last no longer than 45 minutes to 1 hour. After your formal presentation, you can take a break (allowing those who wish to leave to do so.) You can them come back and answer questions or give a brief training session. A sample format for your meetings would be:

1. 7:30 - 7:40   Give the background of your company and it's management. Show intro video if you have one.

2. 7:40 - 7:55   Product overview and demonstrations

3. 7:55 - 8:20   Marketing / Compensation plan overview and initial product order options.

4: 8:20 - 8:30   Product / Income testimonials.

At the close of your meetings, always remind the guests to get with the person who invited them, and let this person answer their questions and give them more specifics on how to get started. This is when they should fill out applications and place initial product orders. Also inform the guests of regularly scheduled meetings and training schools.

* Note: See "Mastering Public Speaking" for more information.

"There is a master key to success with which no man can fail. Its name is Simplicity. Simplicity, I mean, in the sense of reducing to the simplest possible terms every situation that besets us"
- Henry Deterding

Should I Have an Office?

Opening an office is not a prerequisite to being a success in this industry. In fact, the vast majority of distributors in this industry choose to work out of their homes. However, if you have the necessary cash flow, opening an office can be a "plus" because it usually provides a more professional atmosphere.

To help make office space more affordable, many distributors make use of a co-op office. This is where a group of distributors open up several offices in one location. If you are considering this is an option, find a good location, and be sure and allow space for a conference room. It is also important for everybody to sign their own leases, so no one person is financially liable.

Always keep in mind, your success in this industry will be in direct proportion to how well you are able to duplicate yourself. Also note that the simpler your methods of operation are, the quicker your new distributors will be able to learn to be independent. For this reason, it's essential that everything you do be easily duplicated.

Action Points

1. Go back to "The use of the telephone" and write your personalized script (See retail / recruiting scripts, p. 111 for examples).

2. Put together a sample recruiting package from your company's materials.

3. Write an outline for your opportunity meetings.

CHAPTER EIGHT

FOCUS ON OTHERS

T ruly, one of the greatest joys of being involved in the direct marketing industry is having the opportunity to work with others and knowing that you played a part in helping them to achieve their goals. In fact, your success in this industry is dependnt upon, and can be measured by the number of people in your organization that you have helped to become successful. For this reason, I have centered this chapter on how to focus on others and how to help them build a successful organization.

"Half the world is on the wrong scent in the pursuit of happiness. They think it consists in having and getting, and in being served by others. On the contrary, it consists in giving, and in serving others."

- Henry Drummond

Select Committed People

The first step in "focusing on others" is establishing which of your recruits are totally committed to building your company and which are not. I would encourage you to establish a goal of having seven to ten first level people who are committed to your company and group, and who are willing to "pay the price" necessary to achieve their goals. As mentioned earlier, you may have to go through many, many people in order to find seven to ten committed people, but this must be a goal! Be persistent in your building efforts until you've found them, regardless of whether you find them within two or three months, or whether it takes two to three years.

Once you have found a committed person, you should spend your time and resources helping him/her to reach one of the upper levels of achievement in your company. By doing so, you will have helped to give this distributor the two things which he/she must have in order to stay focused on building your company: a **solid income** and **recognition**.

The reason that it is so important to get your people making a solid income is because if they do not begin reaching their financial goals (or see some "light on the horizon"), they may begin to have doubts as to whether or not your company is the right financial vehicle. If this happens, you may lose them all together, or they may become distracted and begin marketing other products on the side.

Focus in on Their Success

This is where your commitment to "focus on others" comes in. Since they have already established their commitment to your group and company, it's essential that you "focus in" on helping them reach their goals. Don't bounce off to recruit someone else just because you have found one of your seven.

"Leadership is the discipline of deliberately exerting special influence within a group to move it toward goals of beneficial permanence that fulfills the groups real needs."
                                        - John Haggai

Remember, successful people can build a strong group on their own. However, with a successful sponsor who is intent on helping them build, they are twice as strong and, therefore, twice as likely to succeed.

Ten Steps to "Focusing In" on Your Distributor

1. Fill out a distributor application with them.
2. Fill out their "initial goals" sheet with them.
3. Help them to determine their initial product order (60-90 days worth).
4. Help them write their "who do you know" list", (p. 197).
5. Determine the number of recruiting videos / packages / brochures / product samples / etc. they will need (suggested minimum is 10 sets).
6. Select their "top ten" prospects from their "who do you know list." Have your distributor get recruiting materials / sample products into the hands of his "top ten" within their first ten days (See Top Ten Prospect's, p. 201 - 208).
7. Give your new distributor set times that you will be available during the following week to meet with him/her and with his/her new prospects. Suggested times include breakfast, lunch, dinner, weekly meetings, Saturdays, etc. Your aim here is for you to do most of the presenting of the opportunity. This both trains your new distributor and takes the pressure off them.
8. After their first 30 days, set up a training meeting for them and their new group of distributors. This meeting should last 2 to 3 hours, and the following topics should be covered:
   a. Company's history or story on how it was formed.
   b. Company's excellent management team.
   c. The timing for the product or how large the market is.
   d. Product details.
   e. How to fill out paperwork (applications, order forms, etc.).
   f. Explanation of the marketing plan.
   g. Retailing your product.
   h. How to recruit (cover the "ten steps to focusing in").
   i. Format for a business opportunity meeting.
9. Determine who your new distributor's 3 or 4 key people are.
10. Commit to do steps 1-8 with them. Teach both your distributor and his 3-4 key people to follow this game plan.

The Recognition Factor

Helping your serious people get to the point where they are earning a significant income from your direct marketing company is by far the most important factor in terms of keeping them committed. You'll also need to give your successful distributors the recognition they've earned for their achievements.

Direct marketing companies typically have a variety of "positions" and "titles" for which successful distributors can qualify. Since achieving these positions is a source of both pride and recognition, always remember the key people in your group, stay on top of their titles, and recognize them on stage at your company meetings.

"I believe you can get everything in life you want if you help enough other people get what they want."
- Zig Ziglar

Consider giving them achievement plaques, pictures, awards, etc. Most importantly, make them feel that you care about them and are committed to their success. Be sincere!

Direct sales leaders who have made it to the top and have earned serious money over a long period of time all have one thing in common: they have people underneath them who have had similar success in their company. For this reason, you should memorize the quotes of Henry Drummond, Zig Ziglar, and John Haggai, and implement the steps outlined in this chapter. By doing so, you will be on your way to experiencing the reality of reaching your goals by helping others reach theirs!

Remember...

• Determine to keep building until you have found 7 - 10 key   people, whether you find them quickly, or if it takes two to three years.

• Keep track of your distributor's title,s and recognize their success publicly.

- Direct sales leaders who have made it to the top and have made serious money over a long period of time have one thing in common: They have people underneath them who have had similar success in their company.

- Successful people can build a strong group on their own. However, with a successful sponsor, committed to helping them build, they are twice as strong, and therefore, twice as likely to succeed.

Action Points

1. Make a copy of "Focusing In" steps and insert them into your Daytimer. Apply these to your key people immediately.

2. Complete top ten worksheets, (p. 201 - 215).

3. Review chapters on initial product / sales aid orders, (p. 107 - 109).

CHAPTER NINE

LONG TERM COMMITMENT

In the introduction to this book, I quoted a *USA Today* poll on what kind of price people would be willing to pay to earn serious money. In that survey, 46% of those questioned indicated that for a $500,000 a year salary, they would be willing to work 12 hours a day, six days a week, 50 weeks a year. However, the poll also showed that 42% of those questioned would not be willing to put forth such long hours. As noted, **people seem to want both a great income and flexibility in their schedules.**

I believe that there is no other industry that offers the potential for the marriage of both freedom of time and a large income like the DS/NM industry. Not only have I personally experienced these rewards, but I have watched many other distributors experience the ultimate goal of most business owners - that is, having both a great income and flexibility of schedules. (Refer to my definition of financial freedom on p. 15.)

This is where the attitude of having a long term commitment (1-3 years) comes in. For you to experience the great rewards of being financially free in direct sales, **you must look at your involvement as a several year project.** There are reasons why it is so important to approach it as a several year project.

First of all, earnings from your direct sales business will typically start out small, but will continually increase, month after month, year after year. Secondly, as your organization matures, a greater percentage of your earnings can be applied towards your financial freedom. In other words, as your organization matures, a lesser percentage of your income will need to be reinvested in your business, and a lesser percentage of your income will be needed to pay off bills and debts that you may have incurred prior to getting involved in direct sales.

Re-invest in Your Business

Your first year should be considered your foundation building period. A good portion of the income that you earn during this time should be poured right back into building your business. **Don't go out and raise your standard of living immediately to match your new income level.** Take needed cash to pay off debts, spend some on things you've been wanting for a long time, and re-invest the rest in your business.

For example, if you received a commission check for $4,000, select a personally sponsored distributor who is committed to building (but may not have capital to work with), and help him/her build his/her business. A few examples of how you could help this distributor would be:

- Help him/her purchase additional products.
- Help him/her purchase needed sales aids.
- Co-op a retail / recruiting advertisement with him/her.
- Co-op a direct mail program with him/her.
- Co-op travel expenses for him/her to go to another city to develop new distributors.

The important thing to do is to use your resources to help the distributor build his/her business, which in turn, helps you build yours. **Commit your first year to earning a basic living and building a solid committed group of distributors. Pour most of your resources back into building.**

The Big Money

The serious money that you will earn in this industry will come the second, third, and fourth years on. By then, the money that was needed early on for building the proper foundation for your business and paying off debts becomes net cash. This is when you can start thinking about paying cash for material possessions such as cars (or even homes). You will also have the luxury of being able to do things like building up a hefty savings account that can grow to even larger amounts over the years. You could set up a college fund with a one time lump sum or fulfill a desire to fund your own ministry or social/community projects.

As one successful distributor once told me, "It's been great to earn big commission checks, but it's been even more exciting to be getting them 30 months in a row."

Consider on the following page what you would do with your income over a long period of time. (Use a pencil to fill in.)

DEBT FREE LIST

TO BE DEBT FREE I NEED TO:	AMOUNT NEEDED	TIME NEEDED TO REACH GOAL
-Pay off my mortgage.	$_____	_____
-Pay off credit cards.	$_____	_____
-Pay off car notes.	$_____	_____
-Pay off bank/personal loans.	$_____	_____
-Pay cash for material needs (furniture, clothing, etc.).	$_____	_____
TOTAL DEBT	$_____	_____

Projected time needed to become completely debt free

_____years_____months.

Things I want to do once I become debt free and have more net cash to spend.

	AMOUNT DESIRED	TIME NEEDED TO REACH GOAL
Fund savings account	$_____	_____
College Fund for children	$_____	_____
Fund my own ministry / community projects	$_____	_____
Pay cash for _____	$_____	_____
Pay cash for a vacation to _____	$_____	_____
_____	$_____	_____
_____	$_____	_____

REMEMBER THIS IS A LONG TERM LIST!

Staying Power

Although direct marketing is by far the most personally and financially rewarding business I know of, difficulties do exist, and you will occasionally experience problems. The fact is, virtually every leader has experienced situations at one time or another that have made him/her consider giving up - and in all probability, you will too.

This is where your staying power will come in! You must realize that some of the greatest opportunities will lie just beyond your most pressing difficulties. It's when things look their worst, that you will need to carefully look for the great potential that lies ahead.

Consider the story of Lee Iaccocca. In the 1970's, as the successful president of the Ford Motor Company, he was credited with creating the car that broke all first year car sales - the Mustang. Under his leadership, Ford had profits of 1.8 billion two years in a row. He earned over $970,000 a year in salary and bonuses! However, at Ford, Iaccocca continually lived in the shadow of Henry Ford II, and in spite of his proven ability to successfully lead Ford Motor Co., Iaccocca was fired by Henry Ford on July 13, 1978.

This could have stopped him in his tracks, but it didn't. A few months later, he became president of the already slumping Chrysler Corporation. In fact, Chrysler lost over $160 million during its third quarter of 1978, and during 1980 they lost $1.7 billion - the largest loss ever by a U.S.company.

"Accept the challenges, so that you may feel the exhileration of victory."
- George S. Patton

However, despite this bleak financial picture, and despite the major struggles which Chrysler was experiencing, Iaccocca saw opportunity. Under his leadership, Chrysler introduced the economical K-cars, convertibles, and mini vans. The company was soon back on track, and it showed strong profits for the first time in several years.

The important lesson to learn from Lee Iaccocca's story is that he would not have had these successes at Chrysler if Henry Ford hadn't fired him. Likewise, you and I must face up to adversities, see past the difficulties of the moment, go back to work, and become successful!

Getting Through the Tough Times

When the times do get tough (and believe me they will), here are a few steps to follow:

1. Get together with the first person upline to you who has had a lot of continued success. Go as many levels up as needed to find this individual and share your struggles with him/her. He/she should be able to help you get past them.
2. Remember and review your visions / goals worksheets.
3. Listen to cassette tapes of successful distributors.
4. Go out and make a large retail sale - MONEY MOTIVATES!
5. Recruit a new distributor. It is amazing how the energy of a new distributor can re-motivate you.

If you have a true desire to become financially free, you will have to have a long term commitment. I can personally testify that it not only works this way, but it really is more fun getting the checks month after month after month!

"Obstacles are built into every opportunity. You have to be willing to work through them to succeed."

- Dennis Windsor

Remember...

• The potential of becoming financially free becomes more of a reality your 2nd, 3rd, and 4th years on. It is during this time that you begin to pay off debts and have more net cash to do the things you really want to do in life.

• Be committed to working through the difficulties that will arise.

Action Points

1. Commit to not raising your standard of living to your new income level during your first year of building.

2. Complete your second through fifth year goal sheets.
3. Select a couple of distributors to pour your resources into.

     A. _____ B. _____

4. Complete debt free list.

CHAPTER TEN

HAVE FUN!

We've already established the fact that the Direct Sales / Network Marketing industry is one of the most exciting types of businesses to be involved in. We've also noted that it is one of the few industries left where you can start out with a minimum of capital and still have a potential to become financially free. I now want to emphasize the fact that the direct marketing industry offers a tremendous amount of fun! That's right, it's fun! Following is a list of some of the benefits you will be likely to experience as a result of your involvement.

Exciting People

The first benefit will be in the type of people you will come in contact with. This industry tends to attract people who want a little bit more out of life than the average person. I call them people with a "maximum life attitude". These people don't want to go home every night and watch television; they want to do something. Not just to be busy, but do things that count - things that have a positive impact on others!

Travel

A second benefit will be your opportunity to travel. Earlier I mentioned that in most cases, you can develop distributors nationally and internationally. This means you will have the opportunity to see places you've always wanted to see. The coast line, the mountains, the autumn leaves - you name the sights, develop a strategy for business there, and then go!

Flexible Schedule

The freedom to set your own pace or schedule is another benefit. If you like to stay up late at night and sleep late the next morning - do it! If you have young children and like to spend quality time in the mornings with them - do it! If you want to take your family on a spur of the moment vacation - do it! If you desire to surprise your wife and take her to an afternoon movie - do it! Work hard, keep your priorities in balance, and set your own schedule from now on!

"I never did a day's work in my life. It was all fun!"
- Thomas A. Edison

Entertainment

Fun company meetings are a fourth benefit of this industry. Exotic places like Hawaii, Toronto, London and Paris are some of the places you'll probably see. The line up may include national speakers, comedians, musical groups, etc. Fun times with lots of your close friends will top off these get togethers. You'll definitely enjoy these well organized events.

Personal Growth

You will also experience tremendous personal growth as a direct result of your business. You'll hear from the best on subjects such as sales techniques, public speaking, motivation, people skills, recruiting, time management, goal setting, etc.

Unlimited Income

Finally, one of the greatest benefits is the financial rewards of this lucrative industry. The sky is the limit in this business. Whatever your goals are, as long as they are realistic, they are achievable through DS/NM. Don't get lost in the money though. Remember what you wanted to accomplish before you got started.

Making it Fun!

The DS/NM industry is basically a people business. If you like working with people, it can be one of the most fulfilling businesses you've ever experienced. Make the most of your opportunity by spending quality time with your organization. Listed below are a few suggestions on "having fun" with your group:

Sizzle sessions - Spend a morning or afternoon with your group at someone's home. Have a potluck, lunch, snacks, etc. Have people share their successes. Make it enjoyable.

Weekend strategy trips - Plan a weekend away at exciting locations - resort hotels, entertainment parks, lakes or the mountains. Take key leaders of your group only and spend time strategizing on how to increase your business. Don't forget to enjoy the atmoshpere of your getaway location.

"You don't pay the price for success. You enjoy the price for success."

- Zig Ziglar

Small group dinners - Choose one of your leaders and have him/her organize a dinner for his/her key people only. Spend quality time getting to know the group. Share exciting stories about your company. Make it fun and believable by sharing some embarrassing moments too.

Entertain together - Whether you are at a company planned convention or at home, go out on a non-business night with one or two couples to a Broadway show, concert or charity event.

Spend the night together - Invite one of your out of town distributors to come in for a day or two and spend the night at your home. Be informal and relaxed. Spend quality time getting to know him/her, and share business building ideas which he/she can take home and implement.

An American writer, Logan Persall Smith, would have loved the DS/NM industry. He once wrote, "There are two things to aim for in life: First, to get what you want; and after that, to enjoy it. Only the wisest of mankind achieve the second." Heed these words and have fun building your organization.

Action Point

1. Plan two occasions to "Make it Fun" with your group.

Event	Who	Date
A._____	_____	_____
B._____	_____	_____

SECTION
II

BUSINESS BUILDING
SECRETS

CHAPTER ELEVEN

RECRUITING THE BEST

If you have the desire to build a statewide, nationwide, or international organization, you not only need to recruit new distributors, but you need to recruit the right type of new distributors. In fact, the better you become at recruiting the "right type" of distributors, the faster your organization will grow.

Over the years, I've watched a lot of people join DS/NM companies. I've also paid very careful attention to which of these people were successful, and which were not. As a result, I've been able to identify many of the traits which are common among successful distributors. Following is a list of the characteristics to look for in your efforts to "recruit the best".

Burning Desire - Deep down, intense desire to accomplish something great - no matter how difficult it will be to reach this goal.

Persistence - Being able to work past the objections and obstacles that stand in the way of achieving a desired goal.

Single-mindedness - The focusing in on one main project or company, not being distracted by or excited to join other opportunities. (This is mainly applicable to distributors who are interested in the full time income potential of a particular company.)

Hungry - At a point in one's career at which this opportunity has to work; backed up against the wall financially.

Entrepreneur - The "I'd like to work for myself and build something of my own" attitude.

Risk Taker - A willingness to take risks, possibly even fail, to reach a desired goal. Someone who is willing to "lay it all on the line."

People Oriented - Enjoys working with others, helping them achieve their goals and reach their full potential.

Dreamer - This characteristic would describe one who has dreamed of owning his/her own business and being financially free, but never has found the right business vehicle or needs to replace the vehicle he/she is on.

Enthusiastic - Excited about what they are doing, using controlled energy to carry out the activities necessary to help them realize their goals.

Self-motivated - Having a "want to" type of motivation; building their business out of personal motivation from within.

Self-disciplined - Focused in on their priorities; setting aside the "busy" things that entangle them and working daily at implementing the activities that help them accomplish their priorities.

Stickability - Having a long term commitment to a project they really believe in. An attitude of "success comes to those who press on after others quit."

Professional Recruiter - A person who is a pro at getting others involved in a project. Someone who is experienced at recruiting.

Promoter - Someone who has been successful at selling or promoting events, product, services, etc.

Loyalty - Committed to the success of his/her organization. Focused, not jumping from one opportunity to another.

Heavy Hitter - Someone who is well connected professionally and who has been financially successful before.

Competitive - Loves a challenge. Seeing the success of others makes them work harder to stay on top.

CHAPTER TWELVE

EXPLAINING MARKETING PLANS

Marketing / Compensation Plans can sometimes be very confusing and technical. Thus, when explaining your plan to potential new distributors, the idea is to make it simple and easy to follow. Most new prospects don't need to see every single title, percentage and override qualification. Instead, they can gradually pick this up over a period of time.

If you are explaining the marketing plan in a "one-on-one" situation, you can use company literature or a notepad (I prefer a notepad). If you're explaining the plan to a large group, you'll want to use some kind of marker board or overhead projector.

To simplify your plan, break it down into specific areas: retail, wholesale, management, and overrides.

Retail - What you want to cover here is the maximum retail percentages at the different achievement levels. To do so, combine the initial retail percentages with the progressive wholesale profits you can earn. For example, if your company's marketing plan has three levels of achievement, and at each level there is an increase in the wholesale profits, you might write things out as follows:

Title	Retail Profit	Wholesale Discount/Rebate	Total Profit
Achievement level C	33%	45%	60%
Achievement level B	33%	35%	55%
Achievement level A	33%	25%	50%
Entry Level	25%		25%

* Note: To make things easier to follow, start at the bottom and work up. In other words, write down the Level A percentages on the bottom of the page, write level B above it, level C above that, and so forth.

Level C	**60%**
Level B	**55%**
Level A	**50%**
Entry	**25%**

Wholesale / Management Commissions - This is the phase of a marketing plan where distributors underneath you are at a lesser achievement level than what you have qualified for. For example, you may be receiving a discount of 45%, and your distributor may be receiving a discount of 25%.

In such instances, the difference between these two discounts (or the "spread") will be your profit. Depending upon how your specific plan works in this area, try to break the figures down into percentages, and explain it from the bottom up.

Level C	45% W/S discount	
Level A	25% W/S discount	
Your profit	20% spread	

Level C	45% W/S discount
Level B	35% W/S discount
Level A	10-25% W/S discount
Your Profit	10-35% spread

Breakaway Overrides - This is where your distributors advance to the same achievement level (and wholesale discount/rebate percentages) which you have attained. When this happens, there is no longer a "spread." Thus, most companies pay what is commonly referred to as "breakaway overrides" on several levels of "breakaway organizations". For example, if A recruits B, who recruits C, who recruits D who recruits E... and all of these people have advanced to your level, your company may pay you overrides on all of their volume. When explaining this, break things down to the most basic terms.

Our company pays:

_____% on your first level.

_____% on your second level.

_____% on your third level.

Our company pays:

__ - __% __ levels.

When explaining the marketing plan, try to cover it within seven to ten minutes. That way, you will keep their attention, and it will be easier for them to retain the main percentages.

Summarize Your Plan

After you have gone over the retail, wholesale and override commissions, summarize them in the following manner:

Retail profits range from _____% to _____%.

Wholesale profits range from _____% to _____%.

Overrides are paid on _____ levels at _____%.`

This summarization will increase their ability to grasp both the percentages which you have outlined and the incredible potential of your opportunity.

CHAPTER THIRTEEN

CONDUCTING "ONE-ON-ONE" MEETINGS

As a DS/NM distributor, much of your time will be spent conducting what are commonly referred to as "one-on-one" meetings. In this type of meeting you meet privately with a prospect and his/her spouse either at their home, or at a restaurant/coffee shop. Although such appointments can center around either retailing or recruiting, this outline will focus on recruiting.

If approached in the right way, "one-on-ones" can be very productive. For maximum effectiveness, be sure you know in advance where you want the meeting to lead, and be sure to bring the materials which are necessary to accomplish your purpose. Typically, you would want to bring along the following items:

1. Sample product.
2. Company brochure } Leave 1 - 3 with your prospect.
3. Company video.
4. Legal notepad for illustrating the opportunity.

To make the most of your time, establish a pre-set time limit, and get to the point as quickly as possible. Always remember to be professional and to show controlled enthusiasm.

At your "one-on-one" meetings, you will want to cover the following key areas:

The scope of the opportunity - You should start out by discussing the general industry which your company is a part of and its potential from a marketing perspective. You will then want to touch upon the specific products or services that your company has available and to show your prospect how these products can directly benefit both themselves and potential customers. If possible, use your company's video to gain their full attention. Cover the marketing/compensation plan here also. Let them know they can make money from this business up front.

Testimonies - Next, share the research which you did before choosing your company and its industry. Tell them why you selected this particular company. If you have been successful, share it with them. If you are just beginning, share the success of others. Let them know where you are heading in the near future with this company and that you'd enjoy helping them achieve a similar level of success.

Support/Training - Inform them of when and where local business opportunity meetings are being conducted, and be sure they realize that they are welcome to utilize these meetings. Communicate how you are willing to help them build. Be specific (see "focusing in" p. 73). Also let them know of any "special events" or regional company meetings that are coming up.

Getting started - If your prospect indicates an interest in working the program, one of your primary objectives should be to lay out a step-by-step game plan for them to follow. Thus, near the end of your meeting, go back to the compensation plan, and share with them the initial levels which they will want to shoot for. This will help them determine what their initial product order should consist of, and what their initial sponsoring goals should be. You should also schedule a follow-up meeting (preferably with your sponsor) and a date for them to attend a business opportunity and/or training meeting.

Note: It is usually a plus to bring your sponsor along with you on these initial meetings. They tend to come off as a third party expert, and they alleviate some of the pressure from you to "close the deal". If they can attend, let them do most of the talking. However, be sure to communicate to your people that you too are adept to the potential of the business. Don't play dumb.

CHAPTER FOURTEEN

USING THE VIDEO

One of the keys to quickly building a large, successful DS/NM business is making the most of your time. For this reason, the video tape is one of the best sales tools ever invented. In 20 minutes, a video tape can tell a prospect about your company, your product line, and the marketing plan. Some corporate videos even contain testimonials from satisfied customers and successful marketers.

Because television is such a powerful medium, a properly produced video tape can actually have more of an impact than a personalized presentation. That's right, it can actually accomplish more in 20 minutes than what it may take you two to three hours to accomplish. Best of all, you don't even have to be present when your prospect views the opportunity!

Salesperson of the Month - The Company Video!

Due to its unparalleled effectiveness, many people are proclaiming their company video to be "Salesperson of the Month". If your company has a strong video, use it religiously. If your company does not have one, you might consider making one.

When using the corporate video, your objective should be to put it into the hands of as many high caliber people as possible. Then, **while the video is doing the work for you**, spend your time doing other productive things.

It's a Numbers Game

As mentioned in an earlier chapter, very few people will pay the price that it takes to build a strong organization. In terms of handing out videos, paying the price might mean showing the tape at least three times a week (if you're part-time) or at least 10 to 15 times a week (if you're full time). If you want to guarantee your success, set a goal of placing at least 100 videos during your first six months.

If you think that you are too busy to do this, but yet you desire a strong organization, you may need to re-examine your priorities, because you are probably busy doing the wrong things.

Duplicating Yourself Like Nothing Else

If you will teach the people in your organization the importance of using your company's video tape, and make sure each of your key people sets a goal of showing the video to at least 10 to 15 people per week, your organization will grow by leaps and bounds. Just think, if you have just 100 people in your group, each of whom is showing the video just 10 times a week, that's 1,000 presentations every week!

Remember...

• Use the video! Use the video! Use the video!

• Show the video to at least 100 people.

Action Points

• Order additional videos to put out A.S.A.P.

• Teach your key people to do the same.

• See "Use the Video Script" on p. 116.

CHAPTER FIFTEEN

CONFERENCE CALL RECRUITING

One of the most productive ways to spend your time in your business is conference calling. In fact, since conference calls allow a person to talk to dozens (or even hundreds) of people simultaneously, they are quickly becoming one of the most popular methods of building and training distributor organizations.

Types Of Calls

Conference calls can be utilized for a variety of reasons. Listed below are some of the most common types of calls:

Two on One - A distributor and his or her upline leader place a call to a prospect. Typically, the purpose of this sort of call is to briefly introduce the new prospect to the business, and convince him/her that he/she needs to take a serious look at it. In such calls, the leader will normally tell the prospect what background he had before joining the company, touch upon why he chose to get involved with the company, and discuss the success which he has experienced with the company. The prospect will then be encouraged to come to an opportunity meeting , or to take a serious look at the information packet which will be coming in the mail.

Group Call - One or more of your leaders instruct all of their key people and prospects to be on the line simultaneously. Each of your leaders can then take two or three minutes and share some of his/her experiences.

End of the Month - These calls are very similar to the "Group Call", but their primary focus is to help people reach new volume levels and titles at month's end. Your objective in such calls is to convey to people the benefits and importance of reaching various levels in your company's maketing plan, and to help your people generate enough volume to qualify for such levels before the month's end.

Company President/Sales Leader - It's always great to hear from your company's president, or from key leaders within the organization. However, because of the vast demand on their time, such people are usually limited in terms of the number of personal phone calls which they can make. A conference call is the ideal solution to this dilemma because a company president or top distributor can personally convey their message to hundreds of people at one time.

Be Prepared

When orchestrating conference calls, proper preparation is essential. Louis Pastuer wrote, "Chance only favors minds which are prepared." Here are some things to consider in preparing to make the call:

Purpose of the Call - Know in advance why you are making the call, and have an outline of the important things to cover.

Have a Leader or Moderator - The more people that you have on a conference call, the more chaotic it can become. Therefore, it's important to designate someone who will act as the "emcee". This person will control the flow, tempo and information being conveyed on the call.

Recognition - Conference calls are a great place to recognize the accomplishments of your key people. Know in advance which of your leaders will be on the call, and try to recognize them, and use their success stories during the call.

Attitude - The "emcee" or main speaker should be "ready to go" when the operator notifies that everybody is on line. Be professional, sincere and enthusiastic. Share how this opportunity has enriched yor life.

Conference Call Services

There are many different companies that offer conference calling services, as well as several options available in terms of billing (i.e. single billing to originator, individual billing to each person on the call, etc.). For further details, check the yellow pages for companies that specialize in conference calling(i.e. *Call Points Inc.* Montgomery, Alabama   800-225-5787), or call any of the major carriers-*AT&T, MCI* or *US SPRINT.*

CHAPTER SIXTEEN

INITIAL PRODUCT ORDERS

If the company you are representing is in the "product business", you will need to have an assortment of products on hand to get started with. Your initial orders will be determined by several factors:
1. Amount you can move in the first 60-90 days.
2. Goals.
3. Capital available.
4. Commitment level (full-time / part-time).

Remember, you are going to be in business for yourself. Thus, you will need to stay motivated to retail and recruit. One source of motivation is in the financial commitment of your initial order. As one direct sales leader once said, "Your initial order should be between serious and nervous!" Serious enough that you have plenty of product on hand and nervous in that you've got to move it to get your money back and make a profit.

Your initial order will also influence the size of the orders which your new recruits place. In fact, prospective distributors will usually ask you how much you started with, and that's where they will start. So if you have high goals in terms of building an organization, keep this in mind.

When placing your initial order, keep in mind the following things:
1. The amount of product you will be needing in the first 60 - 90 days.
2. The markets that you will be targeting.
3. The pattern which you will be establishing for your organization.
4. The importance of putting a degree of "pressure" on yourself financially. (If you are confident of the opportunity, but lack the capital to start at a desired level, consider borrowing to get started.)

CHAPTER SEVENTEEN

INITIAL SALES AIDS

This industry is basically a numbers game. The more people you contact, the more money you'll earn. In order to contact people, you need the right materials to present to them. In fact, you will never want to be in a situation of having a hot prospect, but not having materials to give him/her.

Below is a listing of the materials which you will need to get started with. Order multiple quantities of the items which are marked with an asterisk.

• Product Brochures*

• Applications *

• Order Forms *

• Marketing / Compensation Plan Brochures *

• Recruiting Videos *

• Retail Videos *

• Dealer / New Distributor Kits *

• Company meeting / Training Videos

• Company Magazines

• Company Credibility Brochures

• Promotional Items

CHAPTER EIGHTEEN

RETAIL / RECRUITING SCRIPTS

The following scripts were designed to act as outlines. Choose the one that comes closest to fitting your needs, and then personalize it to the individual prospect. When you are making your calls, remember that one of your main goals is to get your products and/or company video into the hands of the person you are contacting. For this reason, don't "over sell" them on the telephone. Let the product/video convince them of their need to buy the product, or of the financial potential of marketing it. Use controlled enthusiasm, and don't talk too long.

Retail Scripts

Someone you know

(prospect): Hello?

(you):   Hello, Sarah! This is Jackie. How are you doing?

(prospect): Great, Jackie. What's going on with you?

(you):   Well, I've been extremely busy the last couple of weeks. I've opened a new business, and it is really taking off. That's my main reason for calling. My new business is (your company / product line), and I'm contacting several people to let them use it to see how they like it. I'd like to come by (or get together for lunch), and drop some off to let you try for a couple of days. Would Thursday or Friday morning be best for you?

(prospect): Sure, Thursday morning will be fine. (If they want to know details, don't be evasive. Tell them enough to get them excited and curious.)

(you):   Great! I'll come by around 10:00. See you then. Bye for now.

(prospect): Good-bye, Jackie.

"Puppy Dog" Sales Call (Once they've tried it, they'll be hooked.)

(prospect): Hello?

(you):   Hello, Bob! This is Mike. How's it going?

(prospect): Pretty Well, Mike. How's everything with you and Jackie?

(you):   Actually, that's the reason I'm calling. We've diversified into the (<u>your company's product line</u>) and have been amazed by how effective it is. We thought of you a couple days ago and knew you'd like to try it if we felt it was good. I'd like to stop by Thursday or Friday night briefly and drop some off for you to try for a few days. Which would be better for you?

(prospect): Friday is better for us.

(you):   Great! I'll come by around 7:30. See you then.

The "Keep Them Posted" Script

(prospect): Hello?

(you):   Hello, Bob! This is Mike. How's it going?

(prospect): Fine, Mike. How are you?

you):   Great! That's one of the reasons I'm calling. I'm looking into a new business this week, and once I get more information, I'd like to get your opinion on it. It's in the(your company's industry), and everything about it looks great.

(prospect): Hey, that will be fine. Give me a call when you have the details.

(you): Super! I should know more be Friday. I'll touch base with you then.

Friday

(prospect): Hello?

(you): Hello, Bob. Mike again.. How are you doing today?

(prospect): Pretty well, Mike. And you?

(you): Great! I've found out the details on the new business I was telling you about earlier this week. It really looks good. The (your products) are fantastic. I'd like to stop by Saturday morning for a few minutes to let you take a look at them. I think you'll be impressed. Will Saturday be OK?

(prospect): Yes, that'll be OK.

(you): Great. I'll be by around 10:00. See you then.

Local Business - Cold Call

Find out who the decision maker is before you call or right when you get on the line.

(prospect): Thank you for calling (their company name).

(you): Hello. This is (your name) calling for Ms. Taylor (act as if she is expecting your call).

(prospect):   She's on another line. Would you care to hold?

(you):   Yes. I'll hold for just a moment.

(prospect):   Hello, Jackie Taylor speaking.

(you):   Hello, Ms. Taylor. This is (your name) with (use your personal company name). We've brought a new product into the market, and I feel it would be real applicable to your business. (State briefly what it is and how it would benefit the company.) I'd like to drop by briefly on Thursday or Friday to drop off some information to you. Which would be best for me to stop by for five minutes?

(prospect):   Friday, mid-morning, will be find. We're extremely busy so you may have to wait.

(you):   That'll be fine. I'll see you around 10:00 - 10:30 on Friday. Thank you, Ms. Taylor. I'll see you then.

Retail Ad Script

(you):   Hello. John Thompson speaking.

(prospect):   Yes. I'm calling about your ad in the paper.

(you):   Great! With whom am I speaking? (Write down their name.) In case we get disconnected, what is your phone number?

(you):   (Name), what caught your attention in our ad?

(prospect):   (Answer.) Direct your next question to his reply.

(you):   As our ad said, we're offering a free demonstration (or trial use) of our (product). Have you used or tried this type of product before?

NO -   Great. You'll really be impressed once you've tried ours.

YES -   Good. I think you'll realize the benefits of our (product) right away. You can either stop by our office (if you have one) to see our products, or we can stop by your home Thursday afternoon for you to try it. Which would you prefer?

HOME-   My home would be OK.

(you):   Please give me your address and directions. Great. We'll see you Thursday around 3:00. See you then. Good-bye. or

OFFICE-   Your office would be best. Can you give me the address?

(you):   Yes, it is(location & directions). I could see you Thursday or Friday morning. Which is best?

(prospect): Friday around 10:00.

(you):   Great. Here is our number if you need to call us. I look forward to seeing you Friday. Good-bye.

Recruiting Scripts

Someone You Know

(prospect): Hello?

(you):   Hello, Sally. This is Joanne. How are you doing?

(prospect): Fine, Joanne. How about you?

(you):   I'm doing great. Listen, one of the reasons I called is to let you know about a new business I've diversified into. It's in the lucrative (your product) industry. You're entrepreneurial like me, and I thought you'd be interested in taking a look at it. You're not making all the money you can spend are you?

(prospect): No. I've never made as much as I could spend! What's it all about?

(you):   Well, briefly, like I said, it's the(your product)business. This company has some new products that are really taking off. I don't have time to tell you the details now, but could we get together for lunch on Thursday or Friday?

(prospect):   Friday would be fine. Where do you want to meet?

(you):   Let's meet at (location) at 11:30. I can only stay until about 12:30, so I'll bring some information that you can take home to review.

(prospect):   Great! I'll see you then. Bye.

(you):   Bye, Sally.

Using the Video

(prospect):   Hello?

(you):   Hello, Tom! Steve here. How's it going?

(prospect):   Pretty well. How about you?

(you):   Great! Listen, I wanted to touch base with you concerning a new business I've diversified into. It's in the explosive (your product) industry. I've got a company video I'd like to drop off to get your opinion on it. I'll drop it off tonight on my way to another meeting. Is that OK?

(prospect):   Sure. I've been looking for something else to get involved with.

(you):   Great! I think you will be impressed with it. There are a lot of people making some serious money with it. I've got to go for now. I'll see you around 7:30.

(prospect):   See you then. Bye.

(you):   Good-bye.

The "I'm Looking Into" Approach

(prospect): Hello?

(you):   Hello, Mike. This is Bill. How's it going?

(prospect): Not too bad. How are you doing, Bill?

(you):   Great! Listen, I've talked to you before about looking for a business that has serious income potential. I'm looking into an opportunity in the lucrative (your product) industry. If it looks good, I'd like for you to take a serious look at it.

(prospect): That will be great. When will you know something?

(you):   Within the next few days. As soon as I get the details, I'll call you. There are supposed to be some people making some big money in it. I'll let you know.

(prospect): Call me when you find out the details.

(you):   I will. I have to run for now. I'll talk to you in the next few days. See you, Mike.

(prospect): Good-bye, Bill.

Second Call

(prospect): Hello?

(you):   Hello, Mike. Bill again.

(prospect): Hey, Bill! How's it going?

(you):   Great! Listen, I told you about that business I was looking into. Well, it looks even better than I had heard. I now have the full package on it, and I'd like to sit down with you and go over it. Are you free for lunch tomorrow?

(prospect):   Yes. That would be fine.

(you):   Great. How about (location) at 11:30?

(prospect):   Fine.

(you):   I'll be running on a tight schedule. I've got another meeting after that. I'll see you at (location) at 11:30 (day). Bye for now.

Cold Call

(prospect):   Hello. John Thompson speaking.

(you):   Hello, John. My name is Dianna Wilson. The reason I've called is that we've just brought a new product into the area that I think you would be interested in. You're still in the (their business) industry, aren't you?

(prospect):   Yes. That's right. What do you have?

(you):   I've heard about your success in the (their business) and felt that this product would tie right in with what you are doing. It's (brief product discussion.) What I would like to do is stop by for about 5 minutes and give you a quick demonstration as to how it works. Would Thursday or Friday morning be better?

(prospect):   Sure. Friday, mid-morning, would be fine.

(you):   Great! I'll come by around 10:30. I'll see you then. Thanks, John. Good-bye.

(prospect):   Good-bye.

Newspaper Advertising Reversal

This works very effectively on individuals or businesses who have placed ads in the "sales help wanted" section of a local paper. This is a "lower percentage" area of results, but it will provide leads.

(prospect): Hello. John Thompson speaking.

(you): Hello John. My name is Dennis Wilson. I saw your ad in the paper and was impressed by what you said about your company. I'm actually calling on a project I'm involved with, and after reading your ad, I felt you might want to take a look at what we are doing.

(prospect): Can you give me some details?

(you): Sure. We're in the lucrative (your product) industry. We've just brought some new products to the market that are really taking off. What I'd like to do is stop by Thursday or Friday morning for about 5 minutes and leave you some information. Which would be best for you? (If neither time is OK, suggest another.)

(prospect): Friday would be OK.

(you): Great. I'll come by around 10:00. I'll see you then. Thanks.

(prospect): Good-bye.

Business Profile Write Up

Profiles are written on local professional's achievements in local newspapers and magazines. Contact these people with the following script. Since these are usually the type of people who can "make things happen", it's definitely worth the risk of rejection over the phone.

(prospect): Hello. Sally Thompson speaking.

the (name of publication) and was impressed by your accomplishments. The purpose for my call is that I've recently
started a new business in the (your product) industry. Our
company has developed some revolutionary type products that
have really taken off in the market. After reading your profile
and knowing you're a success oriented person, I felt you might
want to take a look at its market potential.

(prospect): Could you give me some brief details?

(you):   Sure. (Go into brief details, but keep curiosity level high. Try
not to let them evaluate its potential over the phone. Try to set
up an appointment to get the product and video into their
hands.) What I'd like to do is stop by Thursday or Friday
morning for about 5 minutes and leave you some information.
Which would be best for you? (If neither time is OK, suggest
another.)

Position Wanted Newspaper Ad

Many people place ads in this section of the classifieds seeking specific
job opportunities. Use the following script to tell them how your opportunity could meet their financial needs.

(prospect): Hello. Sally Thompson speaking.

(you):   Hello, Sally. This is Paula Gregory. I'm with (name of your
personal company), and I saw your ad in the "positions wanted" section of the newspaper. We're in the lucrative (your
product) industry and are looking for someone who has the
ability to work with people and who can build and train a direct sales force. What kind of income level are you looking
for?

(prospect): $_____ per month/year.

(you):   Great! I think we might have an opportunity here for you. I'd
like to get together with you either Thursday or Friday morn-

ing over coffee to discuss this business with you. Which would be best for you?

(prospect): Friday would be fine.

(you): I'll meet you at (location) at 10:00 Friday morning. I look forward to meeting you. See you then. Good-bye.

(prospect): Good-bye.

Bring Them to the Meeting Approach

(prospect): Hello?

(you): Hello, Bob. This is Steve. How's it going?

(prospect): Fine, Steve. How are you?

(you): I'm doing great! I've recently diversified into a new business that has really taken off. It's in the explosive (your product) industry. I thought you would like to take a serious look at it because I know you're not making all the money you can spend!

(prospect): Can you tell me a little more about it?

(you): Sure (Give brief details, and keep curiosity level high. Don't be evasive.). We're having a company briefing tomorrow night at (location) at (time). I think you will be impressed! I'd like to take you to it. Can I pick you up around (time)?

(prospect): Yes, that will be great.

(you): I think you 'll be impressed, Bob! See you then.

Recruiting Advertisement Script

(you):   Hello. Bill Thompson speaking.

(prospect): Yes. I'm calling about your ad in the paper.

(you):   Great. With whom am I speaking? <u>(Write down their name.)</u>
            In case we get disconnected, may I have your phone number?

(you):   Can you tell me what caught your attention in the ad?

(prospect): (answer)

(you):   What kind of income level are you accustomed to?

(prospect): $_____ per month.

(you):   <u>(Name)</u>, let me tell you briefly about our company. We're in
            the explosive <u>(your product)</u> industry. We've just come out
            with several new products that have really taken off in sales.
            (Give a brief description of hot products.) We're looking for
            someone who can build and train a direct sales force and who
            enjoys working with people. Our top reps are earning
            $_____per mo/yr. I'd like to sit down with you and dis-
            cuss this position further (or invite them to a group meeting).
            We could meet at our office (if you have one) or at <u>(local res-
            taurant)</u> for coffee Friday morning. Which would be best for-
            you?

(prospect): Your office would be fine. Would 10:00 be OK?

(you):   That's great. Here's our address. We'll have a complete pack-
            age for you to take with you. I look forward to seeing you Fri-
            day at 10:00. Good-bye.

(prospect): Good-bye.

CHAPTER NINETEEN

ADVERTISING EXAMPLES

Recruiting new distributors should always remain a part of your business game plan. In fact, no matter how long you are in this business, the thrill of watching an organization grow from one distributor to hundreds or even thousands of distributors is one thrill that you will never grow tired of! So continually challenge yourself to recruit someone new.

As stated earlier, most of your organization will come from your personal contacts or the "who do you know" list. But, as you go through these contacts (or possibly even run out of them), you may need to develop alternative methods of prospecting. One of the most profitable alternatives is "effective advertising".

This chapter outlines and illustrates different effective methods of advertising. Besides a brief mention of retail advertising, the major emphasis of this chapter will be towards advertisements which are designed for recruitment purposes.

Retail Advertising

When conducting a retail advertising campaign, your objective is to attract people who would be willing to try your product. Your ads should be brief and to the point and should make it reasonably clear as to what your product is and how a person can go about contacting you to get it. Listed below are a few attention getting retail headers and an illustration of how to personalize your ads.

Sample Retail Ad:

TWENTY PEOPLE NEEDED
to try new patented product that will

_____

_____(fill in your info)_____

_____

Call now for more info!
(123) 456-7890

*Note- To increase your effectiveness, record a 3 minute message on a voice mail box/ answering machine which explains your product. Ask people to leave their name and phone # for additional info. Return their call quickly.

Sample Headers to Use (Always capitalize with bold print, and personalize to your product.)

TWENTY PEOPLE NEEDED
ARE YOU SUFFERING FROM...?
PAYING TOO MUCH FOR(Your Product)?
COMPLIMENTARY (Your Product)

These short, inexpensive ads are great to run in the following areas:

• Newspaper classifieds (discount section - i.e. 7 days for $10.00)
• Free want ad papers (greensheet, penny savers, etc.)
• Church bulletins
• Non-profit organization directories
• Grocery store peg boards
• Apartment laundromats

Flyers

Flyers can also be an excellent lead generator. Keeping your message brief and to the point, design a flyer that you can place in a variety of locations. Door knobs, windshield wipers, doctor's offices, and dry cleaners are examples of where you might place them.

Recruiting Advertising

When advertising for distributors, it's important to target your advertising towards the type of person that you are looking for. For example, if you are seeking part-time distributors, say so. If you are seeking manufacturer's reps, say that. The more specific your ad, the closer the respondents will be to the type of person you are looking for.

Sample Part Time Ads

INCREASE YOUR INCOME
marketing our new, patented
(your products). Reps earning
$500 - $1500 part time. Call
now for more info.
423-4567

NEED EXTRA CASH?
Our reps are earning $500-
$1500 per month working
6 - 10 hours a week marketing
our new (your product). If you
are looking for a part time income
with full time potential,
call now. (123) 456-7890

PART TIME OPPORTUNITY
Earn $1500-$2000 per month
selling our new (your product).
Flexible hours, strong company
support and training.
Call now! (123) 456-7890

$1500 - $2000 PART TIME
is what our reps are earning
selling our new (your product).
Strong company support and
training. (123) 456-7890

Sample Headers

INCREASE YOUR INCOME
$1500-$2000 PART TIME
NEED EXTRA CASH?
PAY OFF DEBT
EARN MONEY AT HOME

PART TIME OPPORTUNITY
DIRECT SALES $2000 P/T
EARN CASH NOW!
RETIRE EARLY!
DEALERS WANTED

Sample Full Time Ads

ATTENTION
SALES PROFESSIONALS
International company
expanding in your area.
We are seeking reps who
can build and train a direct
sales force. Top reps earning
$100,000+ yearly. Call now!
(123) 456-7890

WORK FOR YOURSELF
$75,000+ yearly
If you are not being paid
what you're worth and are
looking for an oportunity that
has: (your product)
  - A Product With Timing
  - National Support
  - Strong Training
  - Car Program
Look no more. Our top reps earn
$75,000+ a year marketing our
(your product). Interviewing this
week. Call now for an appoint
ment. (123) 456-7890

ENTREPRENEURS
$100,000+
Are you looking for a company
that has:
  • National Support
  • Timing
  • Strong Training
  • Car Program
and an unlimited income potential?
Our top reps earn over $100,000
yearly marketing our (your pro
duct). Interviewing this week.
Call now for an appointment.
(123) 456-7890

ACT NOW
Our top reps earned over $100,000
last year marketing our new, pat
ented.(your product). If you're se
rious about your future and are
looking for an opportunity with un
limited potential, call now!
(123) 456-7890

Sample Headers

HEAVY HITTERS	ACT NOW!
ENTREPRENEURS	THIS IS IT!
$100,000+	DOUBLE YOUR INCOME
SERIOUS MONEY	NEED CASH?
PROFESSIONAL WOMEN	PROMOTERS
$60,000 - $100,000+	DIRECT SALES LEADERS
SALES PROFESSIONALS	MLM PROS
$10,000 MO./COMM.	UNLOCK YOUR CORPORATE HANCUFFS
SALES MANAGEMENT	NEVER BEFORE
UNLIMITED INCOME	MANUFACTURER REPS
LEADERS	MEDICAL REPS
STOCK BROKERS	INSURANCE AGENTS

Once again, be sure to customize your ad to reach the specific type of people that you are looking for. When you find an ad that really works, share it with your distributors in other areas.

Action Points

1. Write a retail ad that will work for your product.

_____

_____

_____

_____

_____

2. Write a recruiting ad that will work for your opportunity.

_____

_____

_____

_____

_____

CHAPTER TWENTY

DIRECT MAIL RECRUITING

If handled correctly, direct mail can be an extremely effective means of recruiting distributors, both on a local and a national scale. The reason direct mail can be so effective is that it allows you to get promotional materials in the hands of vast numbers of the targeted audience. In fact, even when response rates are less than one percent, direct mail can still be a profitable means of recruiting.

Experience has shown that direct mail recruiting must be a two-step process. The first step is the "attention" or "qualifying" process, and the second step is the "closing" process. The reason you need to use a two-step process is because **it is virtually impossible to include enough information in a direct mail piece to recruit someone.** Thus, the purpose of a direct mail piece is to arouse your prospects' curiosity to the extent that they will either write or call you for additional information. You can then send them a complete information packet which will give them enough details to make an informed decision as to whether or not they want to participate in your opportunity (see p. 60 for details on what to include).

Developing A Direct Mail Piece

In most instances, a direct mail piece should be short, simple, and to the point. It should tell someone enough to arouse their curiosity, but not enough to allow them to make a decision about the opportunity itself. Remember, all you are trying to accomplish with your mailing is to find prospects who are willing to take a closer look at your opportunity.

Typically, two categories of direct mail pieces are used for recruiting in the DS /NM industry.

Postcards - Postcards are popular with many direct mail recruiters because the lower printing and postage costs associated with this type of mailing allow a person to contact more potential prospects for their money. The downside of using postcards is that you have a limited amount of space to get your message across.

Because your space is limited on a postcard, it's important that you not waste words. You will want to come up with a powerful "HEADLINE", four or five "KEY POINTS", and a strong "CLOSE".

The purpose of your "headline" will be to grab your prospects' attention and make them want to carefully read the rest of the card. To develop a powerful headline, ask yourself the following question: "If I had to describe the most exciting aspect of my company in one sentence or less, what verbage would I choose?" In most cases, the words that you use to describe your opportunity will make a powerful headline.

After you have grabbed your prospects' attention, your next step is to a rouse their curiosity. The simplest way to do this is to briefly outline your company's "key selling points"; you obviously won't have room on a postcard to cover them all. Thus, you might ask yourself, "What are the five most exciting things about my company?" Once you have developed such a list, simply write one sentence about each of the five points. Keep your sentences short and to the point, and remember that you are trying to arouse curiosity!

Once you have peaked your prospects' curiosity, your final step is to "ask for the order". A sentence similar to one of the following examples should suffice.

Examples:

For more information on this exciting opportunity, send $_____ to:

For complete details about how you can make money in this exciting program, call:

Letters - If you want or need to give a prospect more details about your opportunity than a postcard will allow, a standard one or two page letter should do the job.

Developing an effective sales letter is very much like developing a postcard. You need to have a powerful "HEADLINE", you need to cover the "KEY POINTS", and you need a strong "CLOSE". The only real difference is that you have more room to work with. Thus, ask yourself the same questions, and use the same principles used when developing a postcard. But instead of writing one sentence about each of your company's key selling points, you can devote an entire paragraph to each one.

Your final step in composing a direct mail recruiting letter is to "ask for the order". To do so, use a sentence similar to the following example:

Example:

For complete details about this exciting opportunity, fill out the enclosed order form, and mail it to us today!

As you can deduce from the above example, I like to include a separate order form along with a recruiting letter. That way, all a person has to do is fill out the form, and drop it in the mail. Pictured below is a sample order form which you can adopt to your individual needs.

- -

YES, I would like to learn more about this exciting new opportunity! Please rush me a complete information package (which will include an informative video tape). Enclosed is a $15 refundable deposit.

Cash_____   Check_____   Visa_____   MasterCard_____

Name_____Phone_____

Address_____

City_____State_____Zip_____

Credit Card # (if applicable)_____exp._____

Your Name / Your Address / Your City / Your Phone #

Conduct "Test Mailings"

Once you have developed a mailing piece, it's important to test its effectiveness. In other words, before you spend the money to mail out 5,000 or 10,000 pieces, test out 500 or 1,000 pieces and see if they're going to produce the desired results. If the response rate is satisfactory, you can then do a larger mailing. If the response is unsatisfactory, you can re-work your mailing piece, and then start the process over.

When you are conducting test mailings, be sure and do your test mailing to the **same list** you are considering doing a large scale mailing to. Don't test your mailing piece to a list which was obtained from one source, and then pay to mail your materials to another list. The response rates can vary dramatically from one list to another, and just because your test-mailing pulled well in one instance, it's no guarantee that you will receive the same response rate from other lists.

Present Yourself Professionally

When conducting direct mail campaigns, it's important to present yourself in a professional manner. Be sure and use imprinted envelopes (don't rubber stamp them with your name). The sales letter which you are using should be printed on an "eye appealing" letterhead or paper stock. Don't use the photocopy machine!

Sending your mailings via "1st class" mail tends to make a better impression, and typically, it will increase the response rate. If you decide to use "bulk mail", applying "pre-cancelled bulk rate stamps" (rather than having your permit number imprinted on the envelopes) can increase the response rate. In fact, when you use the pre-cancelled stamps, many people don't even realize that it was sent to them bulk rate.

If you decide on obtaining a bulk rate permit, the process is quite simple. All that you need to do is stop by your local post office, fill out a form, and pay a modest permit fee. When you do so, the post master will assign you a permit number, and present you with a booklet showing how to sort and package your mailings.

Co-op Mailings

Once you have found a combination that produces results, you may want to consider putting together what is sometimes referred to as a "Co-op Mailing". This is a concept which allows you to share both the risks and rewards of a direct mail advertising campaign with other distributors in your organization.

To do so, figure out the total costs involved in putting out a large mailing (usually 2,500 - 10,000 pieces), divide the total cost into a certain number of "shares", and offer these "shares" to serious business builders in your organization.

When you have sold all the shares, you can then coordinate the mailing; the leads which come as a result of the mailing can be divided equally between the people who paid for the shares.

Direct mail is a highly specialized field, and it may take some experimentation on your part to find a combination which produces results. However, once you find that combination, it can be extremely lucrative!

Remember...

• Direct mail recruiting must be a two-step process.
• Always "test" your mailing pieces.
• Be sure your materials portray a professional image.

CHAPTER TWENTY-ONE

TESTIMONIAL VIDEOS / BROCHURES

Successful stories sell product! Successful stories recruit distributors! Putting the testimonials of your distributors, who've had great achievement, on a video or in a brochure can cause your organization to explode. Not only can it create a more professional tool to give to potential prospects, but is also can help them to "relate more" to your offer. In other words, when they can visually see other people experiencing positive results, your prospect will be more receptive to your company.

Testimonial Videos

Whether you're doing a product demonstration or trying to recruit someone, the video is probably the most effective tool. If your company has a sound video, use it. If they don't have one, you should consider making your own. What you would want to capture on film are the key distributors who've had both retail and recruiting success.

Here are a few important things to do when producing your own video:

1. Set a maximum of 14-15 minutes as the length of your tape. You want people to be able to watch it quickly.
2. Make it fast paced. It's better to have short, concise testimonies than long, drawn out ones.
3. Use professional video equipment if possible. Either super VHS or CCD epuipment will do.
4. Shoot live testimonials at a meeting and staged ones in someone's office or home. Make sure they're well dressed and that they know what to say ahead of time. Here's what to cover:

A. Name and where they're from.
B. Background.
C. Why they chose the company.
D. Their experience with the products/services.
E. Their success in the business.

Testimonial Brochures/Booklets

A professionally printed brochure or booklet can be a very effective promotional tool also. They are ideal to give out alone or along with a video to prospects. Like the video, they can deliver a more personalized message than a standard company brochure.

Listed below are the important aspects of a good testimonial brochure/booklet:

1. Have it professionally typeset.
2. Cover title should be powerful.
3. Up front information should cover:
    A. The company.
    B. Its products.
    C. Its potential.
4. Printed testimonials should contain same information as videos. Limit to 75-100 words per person and include studio shot photographs.

* Note: For information of publishing customized testimonial brochures/booklets, contact: WINDWARD PRESS, P.O. Box 744275, Dallas, Texas 75374

CHAPTER TWENTY-TWO

SETTING UP YOUR BUSINESS

When compared to opening up a more traditional type of business enterprise, setting yourself up in the direct marketing industry is relatively simple. In fact, comparatively speaking, it's almost like "child's play". However, since your distributorship will be a serious business venture, there are a few basic things which need to be taken care of.

Naming your business - Deciding upon a name for your business is the first thing which most people want to get out of the way. Whether you want to adopt a formal company name, or use a derivative of your personal name (example: John Doe and Associates), makes no difference. The important thing is to use a name by which you can identify your business.

Registering your business - When you adopt a company name (if it is not a derivative of your personal name), most states require you to register that assumed business name at your County Recorders Office. Typically, there is a $5.00 recording fee, and you may be required to run a "public notice" that you are the person who is operating under this assumed business name. Your local government offices can supply you with this information.

Sales Tax Number - When products are sold at retail, most states require that sales tax be collected. If you are representing a DS/NM that collects and pays the state sales tax, this step can be skipped over. However, most programs are structured in a manner which requires that each individual distributor collect and pay sales tax on the products which he/she sells at retail. Registration is a simple process, and forms can be obtained by calling your state Department of Revenue (which is normally listed in the telephone book).

Telephone Line - Once you have established and registered your company's identity, you will probably want to establish a separate business phone line for your business. This will not only add a degree of professionalism to your business (the kids won't be answering important business calls), it may be a necessity if you plan on doing any advertising. For example, many newspapers and publications have policies which only allow them to accept advertising from what they refer to as "established businesses". Typically, the way they verify whether or not you have an "established business" is by checking to see if there is a business telephone listing with your company name.

Three Way Calling - When you establish phone service, be sure to request a feature known as "three way calling". This will allow you to do conference calls with key members of your downline and will prove to be an invaluable asset in terms of building your business.

Telephone Answering System/Voice Mail - Most people find it necessary to either install a telephone answering machine, or set up some sort of "voice mail" system. Many companies now specialize in voice mail communications, and they can offer a variety of services to fit your individual needs. Check your telephone directory under Telephone Answering Services or Voice Mail for a company which services your area.

Post Office Box - If you intend to do any advertising, you may want to set up a P.O. Box. Not only will this help you "maintain privacy" at your residence, the Post Office will forward mail from a P.O. Box for a longer period of time than they will from a residential address. In some areas, there is a shortage of P.O. Boxes, and people find it necessary to go to a "private" postal center (i.e. Mail Boxes, etc). If you take this route, be sure that the firm you are dealing with is well established, because if they go out of business, you will have no way to get your mail.

Business Checking Account - In order to separate business expenses from your personal expenses, it's important to immediately establish a checking account which you will only use for business purposes. This will prove especially helpful when it comes time to file taxes.

Business Credit Card - A bank credit card (MasterCard or Visa) can be an invaluable tool in the DS/NM industry. Credit cards allow you to order products by telephone, and they are a convenient means for keeping track of business related travel and entertainment expenses. For this reason, I suggest applying for a separate credit card which you will only use for business purposes.

Shipping Account - Chapter six, discussed the importance of using overnight couriers (i.e. Federal Express) to send out information packets. Using such services is greatly simplified (and there are discounts available in some instances) if you have an account number. To establish such an account, simply call your courier of choice, and ask for details. (*Federal Express* has a toll free number for this purpose - 800 238-5355.)

Record Keeping - Computers are great, and they are getting more affordable every day. However, a simple Rolodex, or even a box of recipe cards works very well for organizing the names, addresses, and phone numbers of your distributors and prospects.

Fax Number - More and more people are relying upon fax machines to transmit documents. Sooner or later, one of your prospects is going to want to deliver something to you in this manner. If you can't justify the cost of purchasing a machine (and most people can't), it's a good idea to find a local print shop, or secretarial service which accepts incoming fax transmissions. You can then file that phone number underneath FAX in your card file, and when someone wants to know if you have a fax number, you answer affirmatively.

The above mentioned tasks are all relatively simple, and none will require much of your time. For this reason, I suggest getting them out of the way as quickly as possible. Once they are taken care of, you will then be free to concentrate all of your time and energy towards more productive aspects of your business.

CHAPTER TWENTY-THREE

PICKING THE RIGHT VEHICLE

If you want to be successful in this industry, it is absolutely essential that you pick the right company to work with! The reason this is so important is that you will not only be putting your career and reputation on the line, but you will also be asking the distributors whom you develop to do so. Therefore, you should never sign up in any company without first doing your due diligence.

Don't Look in the Junkyard

Picture this scenario: You are in college, and you are planning to ride home for the holidays with your friend, John. This trip home is over 700 miles, and it will take you over mountains, through deserts, etc. On the day of your departure, John calls to say that he has had some car trouble, that he has been forced to borrow another car for the trip home, and that he will be there shortly. About the time you are expecting John to pull up, you hear a loud "Bang!" outside. You run to the front door, and here is John in his borrowed "vehicle". Upon closer look, you see that the car has worn out tires, no spare, it has smoke coming out the tail pipe, it's backfiring, and it has to be push started.

In such a situation, would you dare take a chance that this car is going to get you home for Christmas? Probably not! Yet, many people sign-up in this industry with companies that may look just as bad as this car. My point being, you'll never get anywhere if you don't have a good mode of transportation or the right vehicle.

Finding One That is Safe to Drive

There are several key things to look for when choosing a company to represent. If someone you trust approaches you with an opportunity, and if they have done the research, you may only need to ask a few questions. However, if they haven't done their homework, ask some some serious questions on the following subjects:

Timing - This is definitely one of the most important issues. However, by timing, **I don't necessarily mean that a company has to be a "ground floor opportunity"**. I simply mean that you want to find a company that is still growing, expanding, and enlarging its yearly sales volume. Most companies will grow 50%, 100%, 200%, even 1,000% during their formative years and then level out at 10%, 15% or 20% annual growth. Knowing this, try to find a company that is still coming out with innovative products, services and which is still experiencing explosive growth!   Ironically, many companies that have been in business 10, 15 or 20 years are coming out with products that are setting sales records. So don't necessarily look at the age of the company. Instead, look for one that is growing.

Stability - The other side of the "timing coin" is stability. You don't want to pay the price which is required to build a large, successful organization, only to have it go bankrupt 10 months later. That can hurt! For this reason, it makes good business sense to look for a company that has either been in business for a while with a solid track record, or one that has strong financial backing. If you are considering joining a company that is new, don't hesitate to ask in-depth questions about their finances. A trustworthy company will not dodge these important questions if you ask them professionally.

Products - There are an incredible amount of products and services being marketed by DS/NM companies. When trying to decide what product to associate yourself with, it's usually best to look for a product that has a "recognized need" to it. In other words, you want to look for a product that has a broad based market.

Management - People can look very impressive on a stage, and it is easy to make people look good on video and in brochures. For this reason, don't always trust these perceptions. Do ask questions about the key people running the company, such as:

1. Who are the majority owners?
2. What is their background over the past 7 -10 years?
3. Do they have experience in their current positions?
4. Do they have a successful track record?
5. Are they people oriented?
6. Are they innovative?
7. Do they really believe in their company and what they are doing?
8. Are they committed long term?
9. What are their plans over the next two or three years?
10. Do they want to help a lot of people achieve their financial goals?
11. Can the company handle explosive growth?
12. Are they committed to excellence, ethics, and high integrity?

Marketing Compensation Plan

One of the "bottom lines" in choosing a company is, "Can I make money with it?" If a company is going to survive, the majority of people must be able to answer "YES" to this question. To help determine whether or not the marketing plan is profitable, ask the following questions:

1. Are people making money with the program?
2. What is the top earner currently making?
3. How much are the top twenty people earning?
4. Out of each dollar in sales, how much is paid back to the sales people?
5. What are the retail profit percentages?
6. What are the qualifications to receive commissions?
7. Do people who quit the business block a level of commissions, or are there "roll ups" of active distributors?
8. How many levels deep are commission paid?
9. How much is the average full time distributor earning?
10. If you have 1,000 active distributors, meeting the monthly volume requirements, how much would you earn? $5,000? $10,000?
11. Are there any changes forthcoming, positive or negative?
12. How often are commission paid, and are they on time?

In chapter nine, we revealed that to become financially free, you must earn money year after year. That's why it is critical to pick the right company to pour your life into. It would be a terrible feeling to build a successful distributorship, receive commission checks of $10,000 monthly, only to have the company go out of business after one or two years. At such a point, you would only have just began to experience financial freedom.

Remember...

- A company doesn't have to be a start-up company to have timing to it- just strong growth ahead.

- If you have found the right vehicle, pour everything you've got into it. If you are still looking for the right vehicle, make sure you choose the right one, and then, pour your life into it.

CHAPTER TWENTY-FOUR

MANAGING YOUR MONEY

If you are willi.ng to pay the price it will take to be successful, and if you have picked the right vehicle to pour your heart into, you most likely will begin to earn a very significant income. In fact, your income may increase to a level which, up until now, you've only dreamed about. So the question becomes, "What will you do with the money you are going to be making?"

This chapter is written to try to give you some hints on how to manage your cash flow. This is definitely not legal or professional advice, and I don't consider myself to be an expert on the matter. But since I have had the privilege of earning over $1,000,000 in this industry, I have made a few good choices, some bad ones, and many observations. Keep in mind, my philosophy is to be free from financial debt and entanglements. This is where true freedom lies.

Attitudes

Perspective - As income levels increase, it is easy to lose perspective in the areas of your ego, pride, identity, etc. Try not to let your income change who you are. Instead, use it as an "instrument of good" (fulfilling your goals, charity, etc.).

Balance - Keeping your life in balance will always be a challenge to you. In fact, the more that you have going, the more difficult it is. And during your first year (while you are paying the price) you will probably not be able to keep things in the same sort of balance that you will want to later (your 2nd, 3rd, and 4th year on). The important thing to be aware of throughout your career is the need to keep your family, ministry, work, and social life in balance.

Accountable - I would encourage you to have at least two or three close friends, whom you respect and admire, and who are not associated with your business. Develop a close enough relationship with these people so that you can let them know where you are financially, mentally and emotionally. They, in turn, should have the freedom to make constructive suggestions that will help you keep the right perspective and balance in your life. **Don't surround yourself with "Yes" people. Instead, surround yourself with "What if?" people.**

Your First Year

Control Your Spending - If you have additional cash flow, you'll be tempted to raise your lifestyle to your new income level. Don't! Spend some money on your heart's desires, but pour most of it back into building your business. As long as you have picked a company that offers long term rewards, you'll have plenty of continued cash flow over the years to purchase those things that "you've got to have".

Set Aside For Taxes - More than likely, you'll be paid as an independent contractor, and you'll be responsible for your own income and Social Security taxes. Open up a separate savings account, and set aside at least 30% of your commissions for tax purposes. You may be required to pay quarterly, so be prepared with the cash to do so.

Hire a Certified Public Accountant (CPA) - Set an appointment for an initial consultation to discuss the following:

1. Projected income for new business.

2. Projected tax deductible expenses.

3. Projected tax bracket you'll be in.

4. Projected amount to set aside for taxes.

5. A suggested record keeping system.

Develop a Budget - It is a good idea to have a written game plan as to where you'll spend your money. Keep in mind that during your first year, you are going to be trying to build your business. As a result, you'll be pouring much of your resources back into the business. During this time frame, you may also want to start slowly eliminating debt. Areas in which you should budget are:

1. Living expenses   _____% of income

2. Business building expenses   _____% of income

3. Tithe / Charity   _____% of income

4. Taxes   _____% of income

2nd, 3rd and 4th Years On

Once you have earned a solid first year's income (and have your foundation laid), you can then begin to think long term. This is where you'll experience the incredible potential which this industry offers; and this is where you'll have the continued cash flow to begin doing some of the things that you've always dreamed of doing! Here are a few of the areas you will want to address:

Implement a Debt Free Strategy - One of your major goals in business (and in life) should be to be debt free. Now is the time to begin taking larger percentages of your earnings and putting it toward the retirement of almost all of your debts. These would include loans, credit cards, automobiles, retirement funds, college funds, houses, possessions and so forth. Review your debt free list, (p. 80), and implement a strategy that will get you debt free.

Hire a Financial Planner - Now is the time to get solid, professional advice as to where to put your money. A good financial planner should be a Certified Financial Planner (CFP) and a Registered Investment Advisor (RIA). These titles attest to their acquired knowledge, but not necessarily how effective they are. Check their references and their won-loss records over the last five years.

Subjects you would want to discuss would include the following:

1. A debt-free game plan.

2. 3 - 5 year investment strategy.

3. 5 - 15 year investment strategy.

4. Income allotment.

5. A 3 - 6 month emergency fund.

Continue Expansion - You must always be focused on developing new distributors and upon   pouring your resources into committed ones. Continue to select key people,` and use a percentage of your income to help them increase their organization's size and sales volume. Remember, as you help other reach their goals, you'll reach yours also.

As you begin to experience personally the financial rewards of this industry, you'll need to also be successful in managing the money coming in. By taking this informal information, and applying professional advice, I believe you'll be rich not only in income, but in other important areas of your life as well!

CHAPTER TWENTY-FIVE

WHY DISTRIBUTORS FAIL

1. **No Written Goals -** Doesn't know what he wants out of life and has no direction.

2. No **Commitment -** Does not put forth action.

3. **Only Interested In Personal Profits -** Doesn't care about helping his downline succeed.

4. **No Answering Machine** or answering service. Does not make himself easily accessible.

5. **Uninformed** on how to succeed in network marketing. Has not taken the time to learn.

6. **Doesn't Follow-up** on prospects and customers.

7. **Gives Up Easily -** Usually quits within the first 90 days.

8. **Gets Discouraged Easily -** Lets small problems and inconveniences stand in his way.

9. **Lazy -** Wants to reap the rewards of his organization without working.

10. **Doesn't Handle Complaints** from customers or distributors.

11. **Doesn't Recognize Or Praise** his distributor's accomplishments.

12. **Doesn't Work** his business on a consistent basis.

13. **Blames** the company, the products, the marketing plan, lack of

support from upline, etc. Doesn't realize that if others can succeed under similar circumstances, he can too.

14. **Too Impatient -** Wants to make big money too soon. Is not willing to pay the price.

15. **Takes "No" Personally -** Doesn't realize that "No" only means not now; give me a good reason to say "Yes". Stops calling people the first time he hears a "No".

16. **Can't Cope With Changes** from the company. Isn't willing to be flexible in thinking.

17. **Spends Too Much Time** getting organized and too little time presenting the program to prospects and customers.

18. **Has An Unprofessional Appearance.**

19. **Thinks He Knows Everything -** Is unwilling to take guidance from others.

20. **Doesn't Read** or keep up with what is going on in the industry.

CHAPTER TWENTY-SIX

HUSTLE!

Hustle is doing something that everyone is absolutely certain can't be done.

Hustle is getting the order because you got there first, or because you stayed with it after everyone else gave up.

Hustle is shoe leather and elbow grease and sweat and missing lunch.

Hustle is getting prospects to say "yes" after they've said "no" twenty times.

Hustle is doing more unto a customer than the other guy is doing unto him.

Hustle is believing in yourself and the business you're in.

Hustle is the sheer joy of winning.

Hustle is being the sorest loser in town.

Hustle is hating to take a vacation because you might miss a piece of the action.

Hustle if heaven if you hustle.

> *"Things may come to those who wait, but only the things left by those who hustle."*
> *- Abraham Lincoln*

SECTION
III

PROFESSIONAL TRAINING APPLICATIONS

The following section contains information from commissioned authors to increase your understanding of how to succeed in the Direct Sales/Network Marketing industry. I selected authors, speakers, and trainers, whom I believe are the best in their respective fields, to write on subjects which are a must to understand in order to reach your full potential in this business. Put your concentration caps on, and get ready to learn from the best!

CHAPTER TWENTY-SEVEN

MASTERING PUBLIC SPEAKING

It is Tuesday. There is an Opportunity Meeting scheduled for 7:00 p.m. You are conducting the meeting tonight! You believe in the company; the product is beneficial, and it offers the public many advantages. You believe in the business opportunity. The marketing plan is solid, and people can earn income. You know what to say: you have rehearsed several times, and you really know the features of the program.

Yet, something is wrong. You feel nervous. Though you know **what** to say, you are not sure **how** to say it! You believe in the company and the opportunity it presents. You do not believe in your ability to present it!

Do not be alarmed. Speaking effectively to a room filled with prospects is a difficult task. The major reason is that the speaker usually focuses the attention on him/herself. When this occurs the audience and the message both suffer. To be effective, a speaker must focus the attention off self and focus the attention where it belongs - on the audience. Once this occurs, the speaker has the opportunity to convey meaning.

The purpose of this chapter is to give you specific presentation techniques to allow you to be effective in conducting successful Opportunity Meetings. The benefits from acquiring these skills are: you will speak with more confidence and competency; you will sponsor more people; you will move your business forward; you will be more comfortable and effective in front of groups of people.

Often times, presenters feel "comfortable" in conducting Opportunity Meetings. However, the presenters are not always "effective." The reason: "how" the message is delivered may contradict with "what" is said. For example, the presenter may say how enthusiastic he/she is with the opportunity to share an exciting new business venture; yet the presenter may never smile nor look directly at the audience. The audience may feel the presenter is not excited. The presenter may state how confident he/she is that a representative can earn a reasonable income. If he/she looks down at the floor, steps backward, and says several "uh's", the audience may get the impression that the speaker is not as confident as he/she wants you to believe. What the speaker is saying is being contradicted by the way the speaker is saying it!

In his book, *Silent Messages*, Dr. Albert Mehrabian explains that the delivery is vitally important. Mehrabian states that 7% of your message is comprised of words, 38% is comprised of your tone of voice, and 55% is comprised of your non-verbal behavior. It is not what you say; it is how you say it! This segment addresses the area of delivery. It is divided into three areas: the non-verbal skills (the 55%) the verbal skills (the 38%) and the involvement skill, which ties the first two skills together. Each of these areas will be defined, discussed, and you will be asked to practice each. These three areas will assist you in delivering your message in a professional, confident manner.

Non Verbal Skills

The non-verbal skills consist of posture, gestures, facial expression, and extended eye contact.

Posture

As you first stand in front of the group, you have one shot at first impression. The question you must ask yourself is "What impression am I making?" By maintaining the right posture, you can make the most favorable impression. How do you do that? First of all, you must stand with your feet spread and the weight evenly distributed on both feet. Secondly, you must have your hands at your side. You should lean forward so you give the impression that you are part of the audience. (You want to "connect" with the audience.) This is where you begin. Once you're into this position, you can then move your hands up and out to make gestures.

You should feel the balance and comfort of your stance. If you are swaying, you may give the impression that you're not sure of yourself, not in control. If you keep changing the weight from one leg to the other leg, you may give the impression that you're not as confident as you want to be.

Understand that your gestures begin from this position. Although you begin with your hands at your side, your hands come up to make impactful gestures.

Let's practice! Stand up. Move away from your desk or chair. Stand with your feet spread. The man's stance should be with feet about shoulder width apart. The lady's stance should be with feet a bit closer than shoulder width apart. Once again, you're searching for balance and comfort. You do not want to be rocking back and forth. Therefore, if you set your feet apart, you're balanced, and you give the impression that you are professional, confident, and in control. If you would like to walk from side to side - move into the audience - you can certainly do so. However, it is suggested that once you move to a certain spot, you plant your feet. If your hands aren't being used, they come comfortably to your side. Your shoulders are squared to the audience and you're on the balls of your feet. Once you've moved to that spot, you should deliver a paragraph or two before moving to the next spot, or before you start walking from side to side. People who walk from side to side before finishing a sentence are really burning off nervous energy. They are really "pacing" back and forth. This may show to the audience that the person is a bit nervous and perhaps not confident and secure.

Gestures

Gestures allow you to communicate effectively with your audience. Gestures add impact to your presentation. Your gestures make it easy for the audience to follow your points. Gestures give the audience a visual impression to take with them. Therefore, your gestures are vital in making effective presentations. Your gestures are no more than your arm and hand movements which allow you to express yourself. How is that accomplished? First of all, you need to move out of your comfort zone when making gestures. That comfort zone is usually the area from the shoulders to the belt and the width of the body. Unfortunately, most of the gestures take place in the comfort zone area. This limits your effectiveness. You need to expand your gestures past that comfort zone in order to make impact. For example, you may be talking about increasing your business. With one hand you could actually go from your waist, to your shoulder, to above your head in order to show increase. You may be making the point of expanding your business. You can use both hands to start in the middle, chest high, close to each other. As you expand, you move both hands away from your chest and really extend your arms out to the sides to show "expanding the business." The benefits are involving the audience and allowing the audience to remember what you said. We all remember more of what we see rather than what we hear. Therefore, by using effective gestures the audience is more likely to remember what you were saying. Another hint on using gestures, is to look for the opportunities to use gestures. Look for the opportunity such as numbers, directions, comparisons, action verbs. When you look for the opportunity to gesture, you can use your gestures more effectively. For example, if you are explaining the levels of your hierarchy, you may want to illustrate it by pointing (gesturing) to the front row to show your first generation, the second row to show the next generation, and so on.

Let's practice. If you were to stand up and describe how to use a bow and arrow, you would probably put the arrow in the string and pull the string back from the bow, extending one of you arms; you'd then probably close one eye, slant your head over the imaginary arrow, and move your fingers so the arrow would fly from the bow. Practice doing just that. Practice describing how you would shoot a bow and arrow. Take 30 or 40 seconds to practice that - out loud - using appropriate gestures and describing your actions.

Your gestures should also be meaningful. In other words, don't move your hands if there is no meaning to the action. If your hands are always bouncing back and forth, your audience's eyes will go towards your hands. The audience may miss the message if, in fact, your hands are not conveying meaning. The key point in using gestures is this: the action must fit the words and the words must fit the action.

Practice this in front of a mirror. Rehearse your presentation. Take a 5-minute segment of your presentation, rehearse that segment, and look for the opportunities to gesture. Remember, your gestures should be impactful, they should be meaningful, they should also be above your waist. Depending on the number of people in the audience, if the people in the back row cannot see your gestures because your gestures are below waist level, they are not impactful. Raise your gestures high enough so everyone in the room can see you.

Facial Expressions

Now that you have worked on the skills of posture and gestures, let us improve our gestures from the neck up - our facial expressions and our extended eye contact. Facial expressions are vital. Facial expressions allow you to set the tone and the mood of the meeting. By using facial expressions effectively, you can tell the audience that you are excited about this opportunity. By using facial expressions, you can tell the audience that you are serious about this being one of the best opportunities available.

How do you use facial expressions effectively? First of all, you must look for the opportunities to use facial expressions. Look for the opportunities to show emotions. In other words, if you're happy - tell your face! If you're excited, smile. When you use humor, laugh with the audience. If something funny happens during the presentation, or within the audience, or, if you make a mistake, smile at yourself. This gives the audience "permission" to smile with you. You can also use your facial expressions to show emotions. It's not suggested that you become emotional in front of the audience. However, you can share your emotion with the people in the audience. The best way to practice your facial expressions is with a video camera. If a video camera is not available, you may want to practice in front of a mirror. You can practice by using different types of emotions and expressing them as you speak. Stand in front of the mirror, and describe your all-time favorite vacation. This subject will hopefully show smiles, enthusiasm. You can also practice the other side of emotions, by describing for 15 to 30 seconds the worst automobile you have ever owned. This will show the other side of emotion - perhaps the frustration, the anger, the regrets of buying that automobile. Once again, effectively using your facial expressions allows you to set the tone and the mood of the meeting.

Extended Eye Contact

Extended eye contact is vital for your believability and your credibility as a presenter. Extended eye contact allows you to connect with the audience, establish rapport, credibility and believability. We trust people who look us in the eye. If somebody shifts their eyes back and forth, looking down or away from us, we feel that person is less than trustworthy. Therefore, when you make a presentation, you must maintain eye contact with several members of the audience for a period of time to show that you believe in yourself, believe in the audience, believe in the product, and the opportunity that you are about to present.

How do you maintain proper and effective extended eye contact? First of all, extended eye contact is defined "as holding eye contact with one person from three to five seconds." By holding eye contact three, four, or five seconds with an individual, you give attention and you make individuals feel important. Extended eye contact also establishes that you believe in what you are saying and that you have confidence in what you are saying. Maintaining eye contact for three to five seconds allows you to achieve all those benefits.

You also need to look at more than one person. You need to share your eye contact with as many people in the room as you can. How do you accomplish this? You maintain eye contact with one person, then you randomly seek someone else out and maintain eye contact with that person. Obviously, if you have 250 people in the room, it's very difficult to look in the back of the room and maintain eye contact. Yet if you can find people in the back of the room and maintain that extended eye contact, more of the audience will feel a part of your presentation.

How do you know when three, four, five seconds is over? Usually each time you complete a thought or a sentence, about three, four, or five seconds has elapsed. Then look at someone else in the audience. Remember: share your eye contact with those who want it. Some people do not want to make eye contact with you. Therefore, they will shift their eyes down when you look at them. There's nothing wrong with you; there's nothing wrong with the other person. All you must do is look for the "friendly eyeballs" in the audience; zero in on those people; maintain effective and extended eye contact, and then move to someone else in the room. By doing this you'll give the impression of someone who is confident, professional and in control. Extended eye contact and a smile go a long way in making a new representative or a first-time guest feel at home and feel welcomed. You have just learned and studied the four non-verbal skills to effective presentations. They are: posture, gestures, facial expressions and extended eye contact. Remember, that comprises 55% of your presentation. These skills are the foundation on which the other skills are based. You need to continually work on these skills. One way to work on these skills is to get feedback. Ask one of your friends at the next presentation to give you feedback on your posture, your gestures, your facial expressions and extended eye contact. By getting feedback from someone, you can better gauge yourself as to how effective you are in these areas. Of course the best feedback is to review a video tape of your presentation. If possible, video tape your presentation. Sit down with a note pad and evaluate your performance. This technique will greatly improve your presentation skills.

Verbal Skills

The verbal skills are also important in making effective presentations. This section deals with using your voice effectively and also ridding yourselves of the "filler" words. Filler words are those words that fill our sentences with sound but add no meaning to our sentences. Examples are "uh, you know, ok, like, basically." Those words fill our sentences, yet they really do not convey meaning.

Voice

Your voice is important in conveying meaning. The volume, the range, and the inflection of your voice add credibility and meaning to your presentation. You need to practice raising the volume as well as dropping the volume of your voice. You can practice by using a tape recorder. Set a tape recorder on your desk, stand up, read a paragraph or two out loud, then read the same paragraph in a softer, lower volume. The benefit is that you will learn the ranges of your voice.

You also need to use inflection. By inflecting different words, by pausing after certain words, you can emphasize the words and make impact. For example, the sentence that you may want to convey to your audience is this: "You can achieve this level by sponsoring only five of your people." You can add a great deal more impact with the sentence by pausing between the word "only" and "five". By briefly pausing you add to the concepts what follows the pause. By rehearsing your presentation with a tape recorder, you can tell the loudness and softness of your voice. You can tell when to inflect words differently. You can determine when and how to use the pause. It is vital that you use your voice effectively to convey meaning.

Fillers

How often have you heard a speaker use, "uh" or "you know" or "okay" to the point of distraction? These are called filler words: words, or un-words, that actually add sound to sentences, yet convey no meaning. Other examples are "uh, um, er, you know, okay, like, well, and basically." These words need to be eliminated from our presentations. How do you do that? You must be aware of your tendencies. How do you become aware of the tedencies? Each time you say "uh", each time you say, "you know," you should do something physical - snap your fingers, pat your hand on the table, slap your thigh. This will help you understand when you use the filler words. The best way to become aware is to use the tape recorder. You should set a tape recorder next to your telephone. Record your side of the phone conversation. Once the phone conversation is over, rewind the tape and listen to the recording. You can hear the "uh's". You can tell when you are unsure of yourself as you say "uh, well, and you know." These distract from your presentation. Therefore, become aware of your tendencies. Once again, get feedback from one of your friends at the next opportunity meeting you conduct. By receiving feedback, you can determine how distracting your filler words are to the audience.

Involvement

The manner in which you involve your audience is vital to the success of your presentation. Your audience needs to be involved in your presenta-tion so that each person feels a part; each person shares ownership in the presentation; each person becomes an active listener during the presenta-tion. How do you achieve this involvement? One way is to use names of people in the audience. If you know a person by first name, you may want to include using the names in the presentation. Although you may only know four or five names, use those names. The caution is over-using the names, which may make the people feel uncomfortable. However, when properly placed within the presentation, the use of names can involve members of the audience.

Another way to involve the audience is to use the skills that you have just learned - the posture, the gestures, the facial expressions, the voice. By using those skills, your audience has a variety of ways to be involved in your presentation. A very effective way of involving the audience is getting them to do something. You may want them to raise their hands as you ask, "Who would like to make more money this year than last year?" You may want to have your audience write down the number of dollars they would like to make this year. You may want the audience to write down five of their friend's names that would be interested in this business opportunity. These involvement techniques allow the audience to feel a part of the presentation. Therefore, the presentation has more meaning to them, and they have ownership in it. People enjoy themselves more when they are involved in your presentation.

Remember, you are presenting to the audience, not at the audience. Your audience wants to enjoy the presentation, they want to smile, laugh, be entertained. By using these techniques, you can convey meaning and involve the people.

Your posture gives the impression that you are confident about yourself, the business opportunity, and the product and/or service. Your gestures add impact to your message. Gestures allow you to move effectively, make your points and involve your audience. Extended Eye contact assists you with "connecting" with the audience and demonstrating your confidence. Facial Expressions show your "natural self"-that you are real with real emotions. When used effectively, facial expressions set the tone and mood of your presentation. The volume, inflection, and pace of your voice add impact to the delivery. By eliminating the filler words, you can be more positive and confident in presenting your opportunity.

By practicing these skills you can be more effective in your presentations. The key is practice and preparation. By being prepared you can take the attention off self and focus on the audience. Preparation compensates for a lack of talent.

Biographical Information

Bryan Flanagan, Accentuate the Positive, 3912 Wilshire Dr. Suite A-1, Plano, TX 75023 (214)867-5781. Mr. Flanagan makes his livelihood by presenting ideas, concepts, and opportunities. As a professional persuasion consultant, he works with a variety of individuals, corporations, companies and associations. Mr. Flanagan has real world experience and success in the areas of sales, management, communications, and personal development. He invested 14 years with the IBM Corporation as a salesman, Sales Manager, and National Sales Instructor. For five years, Mr. Flanagan built people and organizations as the Marketing and Development Director of the Zig Ziglar Corporation. Mr. Flanagan's programs are well organized, well presented, and well received. His professional and powerful delivery is guaranteed to involve the audience, teach specific techniques, and transform the "how to's" into the "want to's!" He shows his proven techniques in a way that makes his audience want to listen and to apply the techniques.

CHAPTER TWENTY-EIGHT

THE POWER OF PERSUASION

Our ability to become Financially Free is dependent upon the ultimate value that we can provide to others. You've already discovered that one of the keys to success is to focus on your people (See chapter eight). Successful people in all walks of life have discovered this early in their careers. They've found that the greatest satisfaction in life comes from giving their best to others.

Dennis Windsor knows this. I first met Dennis nearly five years ago, and immediately realized that he and his associates were constantly looking for ways to help others grow and find happiness. The result has been that even before reaching the age of 30, Dennis had achieved many of his lifetime goals.

The important thing for you, the reader, to remember is that the same kind of fulfillment in life is available to you. Satisfaction is not something that is given to a chosen few. Achievers are not born, they develop themselves. You see, it's all a matter of choice. The eventual outcome of our life is determined by the choices we make during our lifetime. Many wonderful writings are available to help us clearly realize that we are where we are today based on our past choices, and where we will be in the future is dependent upon our present and future choices. The fact that you are reading this proves that you are choosing to be a winner. CONGRATULATIONS! The greatest days of your life lie just ahead of you!

Understanding Wants

One of the most fascinating things that I have learned is that most of us really don't know what we want from our life. Many people think that they want lots of money. What they really want are the many opportunities that having the money would provide. Here are several examples:

WE THINK WE WANT	WE REALLY WANT
Money	Opportunity
Luxury Car	Dependable transportation
Fancy Clothes	Pleasing Appearance
Education (degree)	Ability
Marriage	Companionship

Mark Twain once said, "I can teach anybody how to get what they want out of life. The problem is that I can't find anybody who can tell me what they want."

The reason that this may be important to realize is this: since most people may not know what they really want, they will probably not recognize a great opportunity when it is presented to them. You may be very excited about your discovery, but they may not appear to be interested at all. Remember, they see things from their perspective, not yours. Their thoughts and ideas are based upon their past. The harder you try to convince, the more they may resist.

You will be far more successful in providing value to others if you understand the Five Principles of Persuasion.

Five Principles of Persuasion

Before you tell, ask.

I received a phone call at the office one day from a very good friend. It went something like this: "Ron, you are not going to believe this fantastic new business that I just got involved with. Fourteen renowned business leaders are behind these products, and you just won't believe what incredible things these products will do for you." (He was right, I didn't believe any of it.) For nearly ten minutes I listened to this enthusiastic description of this great new opportunity. Never once was I asked what I thought, or if any of this was even of any interest to me.

Sound familiar? It probably does. When we get excited about something, we want to tell the whole world. The challenge here is that **people don't want to be told how great something is. They want to be asked for their opinion.**

Don't tell people about what you are doing. Ask them related questions, and determine how they feel and how they think about the subject. Ask:

- Are you concerned about your family's _____?
- Would it help you if you could save money on your _____each month?
- Have you been reading about all of the _____?
- Do you understand all of the options available from_____?
- Have you ever had problems with _____?

Write out dozens of questions that will get people talking about your product or service. Ask questions. If people discover something, they'll get excited about it. If it's their idea, they'll believe in it. No one can resist an idea if it is their own. But, if you insist on telling them about it, they'll probably resist it. It's your idea not theirs.

Before you talk, listen.

Few of us really like to listen. We'd rather talk. When we were young we were instructed to listen. It probably sounded like this:

- "You keep your mouth shut, and listen to me young woman/man."
- "Children should be seen and not heard."
- "Don't you talk back to me."
- "Did you hear what I said?"
- "You never listen."

Isn't that interesting? We were told to listen. Is it any wonder that we really are not excited about listening now? And yet the irony is that the best way to tell another person anything is to let them do most of the talking.

Don't worry about what you are going to say next. Listen. Really listen. Always be prepared to ask another question. When you disagree with or don't understand what the other person is saying, ask him/her to explain further. Say:

"Really? Why do you say that?"
"Can you tell me why you feel that way?"
"Help me understand what you mean."
"You know, I've never looked at it that way."

Remember, your goal is to listen. **People don't care how much you know until they know how much you care.**

DWTAALTC

I met a man on a plane several years ago who told me that he was in direct sales. He informed me, however, that he wasn't doing very well. He said that people were very skeptical in his part of the country, and they just didn't seem to be interested in his products.

The longer we talked, the more fascinated I became. I remember one story he shared. He had an appointment with a prospect to show a video tape and the woman did not show up as agreed. "I showed her," he told me. "I made another appointment at her house, and this time I did not show up. You can't let people take advantage of you like that."

I must admit I had a very hard time understanding the man's thinking. I had always been told, DWTAALTC. (Don't win the argument and lose the customer.) Why would you ever argue with a customer or a prospect? Your goal is to persuade this person to try your product or to look at your marketing plan. You believe in what you're doing. You know that the other person would benefit by becoming involved. Understand them. Care about them. Never, never argue with them.

Ask for a commitment.

No matter how great your idea or product, most people will not buy or become involved until you ask them. In *The Greatest Salesman In The*

World by O.G. Mandino (which I believe is required reading for this kind of business), St. Paul is reminded that even though he has a life-saving message, people will not seek for it. He is told by the great salesman that he must take the message and "sell" it to people everywhere. Most people need to be asked before they actually make a commitment.

I recently conducted a survey for a gas appliance company. I was asked to survey persons who had expressed an interest in the products but did not buy. There were a variety of reasons given, but over 50% of the respondents included the statement that they were never asked to buy.

A famous foundation once gave a substantial gift to the University of Chicago. Northwestern University, located just a few miles outside the city, received no gift at the time. When the foundation director was asked why Northwestern did not receive a gift he replied, "Northwestern didn't ask."

You may find that you are a little uncomfortable when you "ask for the order." That feeling is normal. Many people get nervous because they may feel like they are being "pushy", and they don't want the other person to feel forced to make a decision. To help you overcome these feelings, please remember:

- They want to be asked.
- They have already stated an interest.
- Your product or idea will benefit them.
- Even if they say "no," they are not rejecting you.

When you ask for the commitment, first summarize the positive benefits that have been agreed to, and then suggest the action that you would like them to take. It may go like this:

"Bill, let me review. You've agreed that you have benefited (or could benefit) from our (your product/service). You've seen how easy it is to use. And you've mentioned several times that you have worried about (similar products/services). Bill, I'd suggest that we complete the agreement tonight, and get a (your product/service). (At this point it is very important that you remain silent. Let him answer.)

You must practice this. As you are speaking with a prospect, make some notes about the positive statements he/she makes about your product/ service. Then when you decide to ask for the commitment, you can quickly summarize his/her reasons to buy.

Believe in others.

I know you believe in your product. I know you are very excited about your marketing plan and what it can do for you and for others. I also know that you have learned to believe in your ability to make it work. It's very important that you also believe in the people that you are communicating with.

People want to do what's right for them. The problem may be that so many have learned to trust their fears and doubts more than they have learned to trust their confident side. By the age of five, the average child has been told "no" 15,000 times. Many of our fears are learned in school. We're told that we're not good at (subject), that we're just not as bright as our (relative), or that we just don't seem to have what it takes. When we have a great idea, we are often told that it will not work. Most of our input is negative. It's no wonder that many of the people we approach may seem negative at first.

Give everyone a chance. Ask them questions. Listen to them. If they are negative, ask and listen some more. **If you have a great opportunity, they may not see it at first, but if you keep in touch, and let them witness your increased confidence and success, many of them will be won over.** Believe in people, and you will soon help them believe in themselves.

Is there more that you can do? Of course there is more! Keep learning. Keep growing. Attend your company's meetings. Read and listen to tapes. Tell everyone about your company. Set BOLD goals. Build your communication skills. Practice. Read this book again. Pray. Believe. You can do it. You will do it. You are doing it!

Biographical Information

Ron Meiss, Business Speakers International, 1156 W. 103rd St., Kansas City, MO 64114. Mr. Meiss is an internationally known speaker on business building topics and has been a national sales leader in two different fields. In 1989, he spoke in 14 different countries on 4 different continents, on topics ranging from sales and marketing to customer service. Mr. Meiss has a degree in communications from the University of Minnesota and a Masters degree from Webster University.

MAXIMIZED PERFORMANCE

I once heard a great definition of insanity: doing the same thing over and over and over...and expecting different results. Interstate Highway 10 goes from Jacksonville, Florida, across the southern United States, through Houston, to Los Angeles. Suppose that you wake up in Houston one bright morning, get in your car, and take off with your family for Los Angeles. After many hours of singing and laughter, you see a sign which reads, "Jacksonville---45 miles". Speeding up won't help! For over 10 years I have worked with people from every walk of life and from every rung on the ladder of success. I have met many people from network marketing organizations who've come to me full of hope, promise, and desire...but stuck. Some are stuck at $1500 per month, and others are stuck at $15,000 per month. It's best to be stuck on the top rung of the ladder, but stuck is stuck if you want to climb higher.

"I've got some real problems... I just don't see how to solve them."

Most of the problems in network marketing can be summarized in three questions:

1. How can Sharon so easily recruit 3 new people every month like clockwork, yet I have to struggle to get 1 ?
2. How can George so easily sell so much of my company's product every month, and I have to force myself to sell any ?
3. How can Jack so easily teach others, then get dedication and commitment from them? Why do I find it difficult to keep people involved, much less build independence, accountability, dedication, and commitment in my associates?

Sound familiar? If you don't have these problems, some of the people in your organization do. How much larger would your business be if they could improve by 15%?

Lee Iacocca probably knows zero about network marketing. Do you think he could solve the problem questions above? I'll bet he could and within two weeks. The point is that THERE IS AN ANSWER! Just because you don't see it, doesn't mean it doesn't exist. It simply means you don't see it. You don't know how many blue cars you passed as you drove to your last appointment. If I had called you before you left your office and said, "I will give you $1000 for every blue car you see; just write down the license number so I can verify it," do you think you would have seen 1 or 2? Probably 36...or 75. You can be surrounded by blue cars and not see them. You can be surrounded by solutions to problems and be blind to them. Were you ever stuck and a friend said, "Try this. It worked for me"? It may have been a simple little hint, and it did solve your problem. I wonder why your friend saw an obvious solution to the problem you found so difficult to solve? I wonder why blue cars are blocked from your sight? If you knew the answers, you might see how to more easily recruit three new distributors per month, or sell more of your company's product, or build commitment in your organization. The next 4 sections are designed to give you some answers. Think about YOUR particular challenges as you read.

The Power of Thought

There are many scientific laws which we should probably know if we want to live a long life. If you fall out of the window on the third floor, you don't fall to the roof five stories above. An unsupported object in the air will fall to the ground. This is an example of the law of cause and effect: your falling downward toward the ground is the effect; gravity is the cause. It might be shown graphically as follows:

```
        cause                      effect
          X -------->------>------>-----> X
```

A similar law also holds true in the mental world. It is shown graphically as follows:

```
        thoughts       action       results
        Y -------->------>------>-----> Y
```

Thoughts are the cause. Results are the effect. And in between is action. If you decide to pick up the phone and make an appointment to give a presentation, the decision to act or not act comes from your head, not your toe or kneecap. I realize that's pretty basic. Sometimes we need to take a good look at the basics. It keeps us grounded in a world of chaos. So the process goes like this: your brain tells your fingers to take action; you pick up the phone, and dial the appropriate numbers. Then, thanks to thoughts, action, and results by Alexander Graham Bell and his associates, you get your result...Phil on the other end of the line.

Different results require different thoughts

Now you desire another result...an appointment with Phil. So other action is necessary...convincing Phil to come over and listen to your presentation. This requires another set of thoughts which you have rehearsed. So your brain tells your mouth what to say, and you end up with Phil at your home for a presentation. Now you require another set of thoughts and actions to get the desired result: Phil joining your organization. If you are a seasoned pro, you don't even realize that you are thinking. It is so automatic. But if you look back to the first presentation you gave, it wasn't quite so easy. Ahhh, the beauty of habits. When you have done an action for a while, you don't even have to think. As the ball comes toward you, you just swing the bat...seemingly without thinking. But what tells the muscles in your arms and hands to rapidly move the bat around the front of you? Thoughts lead to actions which lead to results---a hit or a strike, depending on your skill.

Characteristics of High Performance People

One of the most interesting discussions we have in our seminar results from the question: "What are the main characteristics of high performance people?" As the audience calls them off, I place them around a triangle on a markerboard under 3 categories: Knowledge; Skills; and Habits, Attitudes, Beliefs, and Expectations (HABE). Every group calls out virtually the same list. These characteristics are so ingrained in each of us that we no longer think about them. We just do them...each one at a certain competency level. Take a moment, and glance over the illustration below. In fact, make some copies of it, and do the suggested exercise of rating yourself and some of your team-members on a scale of 0--10.

Characteristics Of High Performance People

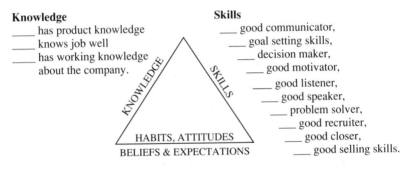

Knowledge
____ has product knowledge
____ knows job well
____ has working knowledge about the company.

Skills
___ good communicator,
___ goal setting skills,
___ decision maker,
___ good motivator,
___ good listener,
___ good speaker,
___ problem solver,
___ good recruiter,
___ good closer,
___ good selling skills.

KNOWLEDGE   SKILLS

HABITS, ATTITUDES
BELIEFS & EXPECTATIONS

Habits, Attitudes, Beliefs, And Expectations
Rate yourself on a 0-10 scale.

___ accountable	___ decisive	___ win-win oriented	___ takes initiative
___ honest	___ delegates	___ happy	___ outgoing
___ productive	___ team player	___ punctual	___ healthy
___ creative	___ high self-esteem	___ common sense	___ responsible
___ caring	___ enthusiastic	___ supportive	___ flexible
___ moral	___ self-motivated	___ confident	___ growing
___ sincere	___ loving	___ ambitious	___ sets good example
___ people oriented	___ tenacious	___ positive	___ magnetic
___ sharing	___ dependable	___ hard worker	___ acts now- doesn't
___ high standards	___ trustworthy	___ self-starter	procrastinate
___ committed	___ enjoys selling	___ ethical	___ good sense of
___ assertive	___ tolerant	___ inspiring	humor
___ patient	___ courageous	___ loyal	___ cooperative
___ rational	___ focused	___ goal oriented	___ hustles

How did you do? Do you notice that some of your associates rate high on most of the characteristics? Did you notice that others are below 4 on several of the most important ones? Do you recognize that all of the characteristics are either thought or they are governed by thought? And that they lead to results?

Increased HABE = Increased Performance

You have just rated yourself in each of the characteristics. You gave yourself a certain number based on how you see yourself presently. You might say you have a "Self Image" for each one. We will address self image in a moment, but first let's see another graphic.

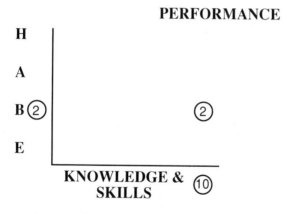

Have you ever known a well educated person who couldn't get much accomplished? They have great knowledge and skills. But somehow they don't perform to the level of the knowledge and skills stored in their heads. Their problem lies in their HABE. Maybe they are a 2 in the area of assertiveness...or commitment... or accountability...or self-starting. Performance is a result of BOTH knowledge/skills and HABE. I can go to school to get more knowledge and skills so I can move toward 10. Where can I go to learn how to climb the ladder on the HABE side of the graph? How can I help people change accountability from 4 to 9 ? Or commitment? Or assertiveness? Forget them for a moment. How can I help me? Are those characteristics learnable at will? Or are they kind of "osmosed"

by being around successful people and hoping it will rub off? How did they get a double dose of it, and I got so little?

Cash Box and Success

I have seen successful people in network marketing in every size and shape, color, nationality, age, weight, and beauty or lack thereof. They have one major thing in common: they are pretty well developed in the Knowledge, Skills, Habit, Attitude, Beliefs, and Expectations required in their particular business. In other words, they rank high on all of the characteristics we just studied.

If all the wealth you will ever make is the result of the Knowledge, Attitudes, Skills, Habits, Beliefs, and Expectations you possess, and these begin in your head as thought, then you might say you have a "Cash Box" sitting on your shoulders. If you were in the military, you know they are big on acronyms...that is, using the first letter of a series of words to form a word. Examples you have seen are NATO, SAC, TAC, etc. If you take the first letter of each of the characteristics above, you will find the acronym "K A S H B Ex". Remember you are getting paid in direct proportion to the numerical value you gave yourself on the rating of the "triangle exercise". So if you ever wonder why Sharon, George, and Jack are outperforming you, all you must do is compare your KASH BEx's to find the answer. They may have an average rating of 7.5 on the top 15 characteristics required for superior performance in your chosen business. Your average rating on those same characteristics may be 6.1. If you want their results, it will require changing a few points on your ratings. But people resist change. We want to remain the same. Then we can go along on autopilot. Did you ever say on January 1, "This year, I'm going to quit smoking, lose 10 pounds, and hold a meeting every night"? Three weeks later, as you smoke a cigarette while eating a piece of chocolate cake and watching the 8 o'clock movie, you wonder, "Why can't I keep New Year's Resolutions?"

Self-Image and Comfort Zones

Each of us has deeply entrenched ideas of how we are, what we want, where we belong, and what we will try. These ideas are called a Self Image. You just rated yourself on the "triangle exercise" above. Since YOU came up with the numbers about yourself, it's pretty obvious that the score on each characteristic is your "self image" in that area. So what? Your performance is married to your self image. You can outperform yourself for a short period, but while you are doing so, you are very upset, uptight, and tense. You will hear a thought run through your mind, "Get back to where you belong! Fast!" Let's take a quick trip back to high school. It is a great way to examine how thoughts lead to action which leads to results. It is also a great way to see that the mental rules don't change...just the game in which we play.

The Way We Were

SELF-IMAGE	PERFORMANCE	
l	l	A
l	l	
C	l	l	C
l	l	
l	l	F

Let's say you were a "C" student in school. For some reason, you made an "A" on a test one day. The first thought which ran through you head was, "Boy, am I a smart person!" The next thought through your head was, "You know, I can flunk the next 2 tests and still get my "C" for the six-weeks." Now, I'm sure YOU didn't do that, but you knew a lot of kids who did. (By the way, "B" students do the same thing with "A's" and "C's" to get their "B" each six-weeks.) Now let's suppose the "C" student gets an "F" on a test. His first thought is, "Dad is going to kill me!" So he goes to his room to study for tomorrow's test, and the phone rings. His best friend says, "Hey man, wanna go to the movies tonight?" He answers hurriedly, "No way. I'm gonna be up all night. I've gotta get an "A" on this test to-morrow, or Dad will blitz out, and I won't see a movie til summer!" Where does all the drive and energy (MOTIVATION) come from to make this kid stay up all night studying? And now he has to get creative to find a person to help him learn enough Algebra to make an "A" tomorrow. After that he can relax and slow down. And sure enough, he gets his "A". The next thought is, "Whew. That was close. Now I can get down to some serious partying. 'Hey Sue, whatcha doin' tonight?'"

The Way We Are Today

	SELF-IMAGE		PERFORMANCE	
	1		1	2000
	1		1	
1500	1		1	1500
	1		1	
	1		1	900

If you make $1500 per month, you will say, "Oh, I make about $1500 a month. Yep, it's just like me." (This analogy holds true if you make $15,000 per month...or more). You have a bad month, and you make $900. Your first thought is, "I could lose the house! I better get to work." You will now work 18 hours per day, and call on people you never had the courage to call on before (drive and energy and creativity seemingly come out of nowhere to assist you). The next month you make $2000. "Let's see...$2000 this month plus $900 last month...that's $1450 average. Whew. Almost lost the house. That was a close one. But now I can slow down and get back to normal. "You coast along at "normal" for a few months, and suddenly the big deal comes through...the one you always hoped for. You make $2000. First thought---"All right...2 grand. Now if I do this every month, that'll be...$24,000 this year. Honey, let's go test drive that new Cadillac. We're rolling now!!!" The next thought---"You know, I've really been working hard, haven't spent much time with the kids. I think we should go to Orlando and introduce the kids to Mickey and Goofey." And the next month you earn $900. "Am I doomed to stay at $1500?"

The Way It Will Be

The key is to change the self-image from $1500 per month to $2000 per month. If you can do that, then you don't have to try hard, kill yourself, and have all the stress and anxiety. You will then go out and act like the AD-VANCED you...and free-flowingly, calmly make $2000. Your self-image controls performance. How can you change that subconscious self-image to a higher standard... a higher expectancy level? Remember the "triangle exercise" and the "Characteristics of High Performance People"? Please note when you look at your self-rating, that you were not born at that number. Each of us has arrived at each rating number over the years through a process of growth. Some of that growth has been intentional. Most of it has been by ACCIDENT as you unconsciously absorbed the characteristics of your parents, teachers, minister-priests-rabbis, co-workers, bosses, the 6 o'clock newscasters, and other role models. If you would like to take control of the process in the future, there are several options from which to choose. Which option is best? "What works" is the best - the single option or combination of options which grabs your heart and mind and causes you to move to your destination the quickest.

Option Zero

You can accept the way you are and the way things are, and settle for "the way life is"...then your epitaph can read, "Died age 18, buried age 71". That's an option, but not a very good one. Fifty three or so years is too long to not participate in the adventure.

Option Zero + a little

Trial & Error---trying to invent the way yourself, with little or no knowledge of network marketing. Never listening. Being totally un-teachable. (Forget it! You won't live long enough.)

Option One

To gain the knowledge and skills required for your particular business, it is imperative to attend every company sponsored training program and quick-start session. Your company has spent a great deal of time and money to help you, I'm sure. You and your organization should "camp out" at these meetings. If you gain one new idea, remember "new thoughts=new action=new results".

Option Two

Another option is to read business building books and listen to cassette tapes. The correct thoughts which lead to the correct actions which lead to the results you want, have been put on paper and tape. THE ANSWERS TO THE QUESTIONS YOU HAVE DO EXIST. Ask one of the successful people in "Option Three" which books and tapes are the best. Then, be creative and go find some on your own.

Option Three

Surround yourself with successful people in your business. As my father used to say, "If you want to make $50,000, don't hang out with people making $20,000. They don't know how." Not only do they not know how, but you will unconsciously pick up their KASH BEx ratings and make them part of you. So if you want to be a good recruiter/retailer, hang out with great recruiters/retailers, and pick their brains. Watch what the good ones do, and copy them.

Option Four

There is a wealth of information to be gained by attending "outside" seminars. Some companies have compiled vast amounts of research and teach it very well in a short time. When you find one with practical, useful, applicable material, it can be a gold mine. The major challenge with most "outside" seminars, is that they are usually generalized and non-specific to the needs of network marketers. You may need someone with experience in your business to go with you to translate the information into practical, usable ideas. If you are the experienced one, you might find going to such a seminar mentally stimulating for you and very rewarding to your group. If they find a missing piece to their individual puzzles, they will take action, which means results, which means money. Sometimes people HEAR an idea from an outside "expert" (which you told them 100 times!).

Okay, you know what to do...

Please be assured that the answers to doubling your income in network marketing are neatly printed between the covers of THIS book. If you will put these priciples to work, the next book you will need to read will be entitled, "*Hawaiian Island Hideaways*". The ultimate question is, **"Will you use what you have learned?"**

Biographical Information

Jim Hoyt, President, Producers Group Incorporated, P.O. Box 833120, Richardson, TX 75083, (214)644-2691. Mr. Hoyt has spoken to sales leaders in the U.S., Canada, England and Europe on the topics of self-esteem, self-confidence and performance skills. His seminars have reached over 30,000 people of which 20,000 were engaged in the direct sales / network marketing industry. He himself built a network marketing organization which paid for his college education. Mr. Hoyt's presentations are specifically designed for self-employed people who have a burning desire to reach their full potential.

CHAPTER THIRTY

BRINGING OUT THE BEST IN PEOPLE

Have you ever wondered at the way certain people bring out the best in others? We have all known them - chief executives, coaches, parents. They seem to possess a knack for inspiring people. And this remarkable skill in the art of motivation makes them successful at almost everything they do.

Virtually everyone is called upon to inspire others in one situation or another. And almost everyone is capable of rising to the occasion because most often motivators are made - not born.

Here are key principles that can be mastered by anyone with the desire to inspire others - and in doing so experience one of life's greatest joys.

Expect the best. People who like people and who believe those they lead have the best of intentions will get the best from them.

In their famous study, Robert Rosenthal, a Harvard psychologist, and Lenore Jacobson, a South San Francisco school principal, found that raising a teacher's expectations of students tended to improve the children's performances. At the start of a fall term, elementary school teachers were assigned a number of pupils designated as "spurters"- children most likely to have academic gain. In fact, they had been chosen at random.

Tested at the end of the year, the pupils whom the teachers thought had the most potential had increased their I.Q. more than had their classmates. The teachers described them as happier, more curious, more affectionate than average, and as having a better chance of success in later life. Because the teachers had been led to expect more of certain students, those children may have come to expect more of themselves.

Study other people's needs. Too many leaders who see motivation as mere backslapping and pep talks ignore this essential early step. We must ask questions about what people believe, what they love, what they hate. We must say, "Tell me about yourself." Real leaders know that if they listen long enough, people will explain how they can be motivated.

A professor told me how his department chairman called him in one day and explained that his salary couldn't be raised, but that he would be given tenure a year early and a reduced teaching load.

Explained the professor: "What the chairman didn't know was that tenure was no carrot at all for me. As to reducing my load, if he had been paying attention, he would have realized that I loved teaching so much I would have paid for the privilege. If he had taken the trouble to find out more about my needs, he could have been more successful in motivating me."

Set high standards. In successful families, as well as the best-run companies, leaders tolerate a considerable amount of individuality. But they insist upon certain core beliefs as well as high standards.

An art teacher I know rotates among five different schools each week. "Do you know what school has the worst morale?" she asked. "It's the one where the principal tries hardest to be popular with everyone. He'll say things to us like, 'Don't bother to come to the school program tonight if it's not convenient.' Such a laissex-faire attitude conveys the message, 'This school is not worth caring about.'"

Leadership methods seem to vary greatly, but one constant among successful motivators is a devotion to ideas - and superior work.

Create an environment where failure is not fatal. A woman with vast experience in politics, who had observed many great public figures, once said to me, "It is an ability to fail that makes for lasting success."

That lesson was learned early by a young black woman who made her debut as New York City's Town Hall. She wasn't ready, and the critics flayed her. Members of her church had started her on her career by pooling their nickels and dimes for a fund for Marian Anderson, and after the New York debacle, she couldn't face them.

The singer's depression lasted for more than a year, in spite of her mother's efforts to persuade her to have faith that she still had a gift. Looking back, the great vocalist said, "Whatever is in my voice, faith has put it there. Faith and my mother's words: 'Grace must come before greatness.' "

The best managers expect their people to make mistakes and, instead of replacing staff constantly, recognize that it is more efficient to teach people how to learn from their mistakes. A motivator knows that the fear of failure can destroy creativity and initiative.

Use role models to encourage success. Great persuaders are good storytellers, for they know that we are more easily influenced by individualized experiences than by general principles.

Looking back on the dinner conversations I had when I was growing up, I see how effectively my father used heroes to motivate his sons. A thoughtful, soft-spoken man, he would comment on the people in our town whom he admired : a businessman going to law school at night, or a young farmer taking correspondence classes. Both my brother and I went on to get doctoral degrees, and I see now how strongly our father propelled us toward success. He did what all effective teachers do - he gave us strong values by holding up real people who embodied those values.

Recognize and applaud achievement. The complaint employees most often express is this: "I never get feedback from the boss - except when something goes wrong." In *The One Minute Manager*, Kenneth Blanchard and Spencer Johnson advise: catch your subordinates doing something right, then praise them immediately.

Taking the time to thank people who help us is a basic courtesy that should apply in all human relations. We all want to be appreciated, and when someone genuinely thanks us, we will follow that person a long way. "The applause of a single human being," said the English critic Samuel Johnson, "is of great consequence."

Place a premium of collaboration. What is it about some leaders that enables them to so construct their group that there is always high esprit de corps and a tight allegiance to one another?

In his book *American Caesar*, William Manchester analyzes the fierce loyalty that Douglas MacArthur elicited from his men during World War I. The key: "He adored them in return." For all his egomania, MacArthur was able to convey his loyalty to his men.

Good leaders do more than build allegiance to themselves - they also build into the organization an allegiance to one another. In the best organizations people will take responsibility for ensuring high standards. A friend bought a factory a few years ago. "Among the employees," he said, "I found a clique of old-timers who consistently turned out the best work. When they got together at coffee breaks, they would show one another their work, scoff at something poorly done and admire what was good."

"There was a group pride functioning here - it was important that they not allow anyone among them to fail. They all did a better job because of the inner competition and loyalty." That factory owner had learned the important lesson of allowing group morale to do much of his work for him.

The ultimate leaders develop followers who will surpass them. Runners will become coaches and train other athletes who will break their records. Executives will motivate subordinates so successfully that they will become their superiors. And parents, in their devotion to a child, will pull him or her up beside them - and then encourage the child to go even higher.

When Harry and Ada Mae Day had their first child, they traveled 225 miles from their ranch to El Paso for the delivery, and Ada Mae brought her baby, Sandra, home to a difficult life. The four-room adobe house had no running water and no electricity. There was no school within driving distance.

But the Days did not allow themselves to be limited by their surroundings. Harry had been forced by his father's death to take over the ranch rather than enter Stanford University, but he never gave up hope that his daughter would someday study there. Sandra's mother first taught her at home, and also saw to it that the house was stocked with newspapers, magazines and books. One summer the Days took their children to all the state capitals west of the Mississippi.

Sandra did go to Stanford, to law school, and became the first woman

Justice on the U.S. Supreme Court. On the day of her swearing in, the family was there. "She looked around, saw us and locked her eyes right into ours," said her brother, Alan. "That's when the tears started falling."

What motivates a woman like Sandra Day O'Connor? Intelligence, of course, and inner drive. But much of the credit goes to a determined ranch mother sitting in her adobe house, reading to her children by the hour, and who, with her husband, scampered up the stairways of capitol domes, their children in tow.

SECTION IV

SAMPLE WORKSHEETS

MY INITIAL GOALS

	1st TWO WEEKS	1st MONTH	1st 90 DAYS	1st SIX MONTHS	1st YEAR	
APPLICATION COMPLETED						
AMOUNT OF INITIAL ORDER						
WHO DO YOU KNOW LIST						
TOP TEN SELECTED						
PEOPLE CONTACTED						
PRODUCT/ OPPORTUNITY PRESENTATIONS						
OPPORTUNITY MEETINGS ATTENDED WITH GUEST						
VIDEOS PLACED						
DISTRIBUTORS SPONSORED						
PRODUCT SOLD						
WHOLESALE VOLUME MOVED						
TITLE REACHED						
INCOME EARNED						

2ND THROUGH 5TH YEAR GOAL SHEET

194

2nd Year Goals
My second year in business will be from _____ to _____. I am committed to applying the principles/action points outlined in this book and to paying the price it will take to reach the goals listed below.

1. I will reach the_____ distributor level.

2. I will have _____ front line distributors.

3. Personally sponsored distributors who've reached _____ level _____;

     _____ level _____; _____ level _____.

4. Total in my organization will be _____.

5. I will earn _____ my second year.

6. Total income I will have earned my first two years will be _____.

7. I will be debt free in these areas _____, _____, _____.

8. My goal for my savings account will be _____.

9. I'm going to take a _____ day vacation to _____.

10. _____.

11. _____.

_____   _____
Signed   Date

3rd Year Goals
My third year in business will be from _____ to _____. I am committed to applying the principles/action points outlined in this book and to paying the price it will take to reach the goals listed below.

1. I will reach the_____ distributor level.

2. I will have _____ front line distributors.

3. Personally sponsored distributors who've reached _____ level _____;

     _____ level _____; _____ level _____.

4. Total in my organization will be _____.

5. I will earn _____ my third year.

6. Total income I will have earned my first three years will be _____.

7. I will be debt free in these areas _____, _____, _____.

8. My goal for my savings account will be _____.

9. I'm going to take a _____ day vacation to _____.

10. _____.

11. _____.

_____   _____
Signed   Date

4th Year Goals

My fourth year in business will be from _____ to _____. I am committed to applying the principles/action points outlined in this book and to paying the price it will take to reach the goals listed below.

1. I will reach the_____ distributor level.

2. I will have _____ front line distributors.

3. Personally sponsored distributors who've reached _____ level _____;

   _____ level _____; _____ level _____.

4. Total in my organization will be _____.

5. I will earn _____ my fourth year.

6. Total income I will have earned my first four years will be _____.

7. I will be debt free in these areas _____, _____, _____.

8. My goal for my savings account will be _____.

9. I'm going to take a _____ day vacation to _____.

10. _____.

11. _____.

_____ _____
Signed   Date

5th Year Goals

My fifth year in business will be from _____ to _____. I am committed to applying the principles/action points outlined in this book and to paying the price it will take to reach the goals listed below.

1. I will reach the_____ distributor level.

2. I will have _____ front line distributors.

3. Personally sponsored distributors who've reached _____ level _____;

   _____ level _____; _____ level _____.

4. Total in my organization will be _____.

5. I will earn _____ my fifth year.

6. Total income I will have earned my first five years will be _____.

7. I will be debt free in these areas _____, _____, _____.

8. My goal for my savings account will be _____.

9. I'm going to take a _____ day vacation to _____.

10. _____.

11. _____.

_____ _____
Signed   Date

WHO DO YOU KNOW?

Throughout this book, I've made mention of the fact that building a DS/NM organization is basically a "numbers game", and the more people that you expose your opportunity to, the more success you will achieve. The following section has been designed to help you develop a large prospect list to which you can introduce your business. You will want to be continually updating and adding to this list.

Centers of Influence - People who know you well and who are interested in your success. (You may not consider all of these people "prospects", but you can use these people as a source of referrals who you do not know.)

Home Expenditures - You pay these people money every month.
Grocer
Baker
Butcher
Dairyman
Laundryman
Electric Company
Gas Company
Water Company
Dry Cleaners

Home Ownership and Maintenance - Who do you know because you own it? Who do you depend on for its maintenance?
Real Estate Broker
Contractor
Foreman or Contractor
City Engineer

Landscape Man
Architect
Painter
Insurance Salesman
Interior Decorator
Plumber
Electrician
Appliance Salesman
Lumber Dealer
Cabinet Maker

Adults You Know Through Your Children's Activities
School Teachers
Music Teachers
Voice Teachers
Band Instructors
School Principals
Summer Camp Teachers
Swimming Teachers
Dancing Teachers
Parents of your Children's Friends
School Equipment Dealers
School Board Members
Sunday School Teachers

Professional People You Know
Doctors
Lawyers
Dentists
Bankers
Chiropractors
Naturalists
Novelists
Optician
Osteopath
Surgeon

Church, Club, Fraternities, Civic Affairs - People you know through these organizations.

Church
Luncheon Club
Country Club
Y.M.C.A.
Red Cross
Chamber of Commerce
American Legion
Veterans of Foreign Wars
Community Chest
Trade Organizations

Neighbors and People You Know Socially - People with whom you go to the theatre, play bridge, have evening visits, or take in sports events.

Previous Business Associates or Competitors - Owners of the business where you formerly worked - the executives or employees. You may also recall some competitors in your former line of work.

Your Spouse's Activities - Husbands or wives of leaders and members of your spouse's clubs.
Book Club
Bridge Club
PTA
Alumni Associations
Sorority or Fraternity
Church Organizations
Garden Club
Women's or Men's Clubs

Hobbies and Sports - Whom do you know through your hobbies?
Fishing
Golf
Tennis
Bowling
Music
Public Speaking
Photography
Work Shop
Football

Book Collecting
Stamp Collecting
Hunting
Baseball
Softball
Riding
Painting

Your Car Purchase and Maintenance - Names of people you know through purchase or maintenance of your car.
Car Dealer
Service Manager
Salesman
Tire Dealers
Service Station Operators
Car Insurance Salesman
Battery Man
Finance Company

School and College - People you know because you went to a certain school, high school, or college. If you attended recently, names should come to mind easily. If it was a long time ago, it may require reference to old records, or year books.

DEVELOPING YOUR "TOP TEN" PROSPECT LIST

After you have completed your "Who Do You Know" list, you will want to contact your most "qualified" prospects as quickly as possible. Thus, go back through your list of names, and evaluate the strength of each person by putting an asterisk by their name each time they match one of the key characteristics which you are looking for in a prospective distributor.

When completed, your list will look similar to this:

********	Tom Smith
****	Bill Jones
******	Robyn Walters
**	Brad Connors
*****	Jill Thompson
******	Dianna Henderson
***	Paul Edwards

Once you have evaluated your list of names, turn to your "Top Ten" prospect list, (See p. 208) and transfer the ten names with the most asterisks to this list. Then get together with your sponsor and develop a game plan to recruit these people. Timing here is important! Get together with these people as quickly as possible (during the next two weeks).

When you contact your "Top Ten" prospects, do one of the following:

1. Set up a meeting with them and your sponsor.
2. Take them to an opportunity meeting.
3. Meet with them one-on-one (see p. 99 for format).
4. Drop off or send them a video and brochure packet.

As you sign up your distributors, you need to focus in on them. This again, is where you'll help them try to meet with their top prospects. Use the "focusing in" outline (p. 73) to help them build their group.

Finally, as your personally sponsored distributor organization grows, keep track of all their key people on a "Key Leaders" page (See sample, p. 216-217). Remember to keep photocopies of the worksheets in your daytimer.

EXAMPLE OF
TOP TEN
PROSPECTS

NAME	DAY / NIGHT PHONE #'S	ADDRESS
Phil Jones	123-4567/765-4321	123 Bay Ave.
Kay Lucas	123-4567/765-4321	123 Bay Ave.
Shelly Williams	123-4567/765-4321	123 Bay Ave.

EXAMPLE OF
TOP TEN
DISTRIBUTORS

NAME	DAY / NIGHT PHONE #'S	ADDRESS
Sally Evans	123-4567/765-4321	123 Bay Ave.
Paul Thomas	123-4567/765-4321	123 Bay Ave.
Jean Butler	123-4567/765-4321	123 Bay Ave.

PRODUCT DEMO	VIDEO PACKET SENT	SEEN VIDEO	ATTENDED MEETING	FOLLOW-UP PHONE CALL	FOLLOW-UP MEETING WITH SPONSOR	COMPLETED APPLICATION	INITIAL ORDER	COMPLETED "WHO DO YOU KNOW" LIST		
	√	√		√	√	√	$800	√		
√		√	√	√	√	√	$3000			
√		√	√	√	√	√	$250	√		

SS# / DIST #	INITIAL ORDER	TITLE	MONTHLY INCOME GOAL	COMPLETED FOCUSING-IN STEPS	SIGNED 3-4 KEY PEOPLE	
123-45-6789	$1800	Level C	$6000	√	√	
123-45-6789	$1200	Level B	$4000	√	√	
123-45-6789	$600	Level A	$2000	√	√	

EXAMPLE OF
TOP TEN'S
PROSPECTS

DISTRIBUTOR	JAY EDWARDS	LORI THOMAS
NAME	BOB HILL	PAULA JOHNSON
PHONE #	(123) 456-7890	(123) 456-7890
INFO (Seen video, product, occupation)	REAL ESTATE BROKER seen video, has questions	OWNS CLOTHING STORE seen products, very interested
NAME	RAY SMITH	TOM PEDERSON
PHONE #	(123) 456-7890	(123) 456-7890
INFO (Seen video, product, occupation)	PUBLIC SPEAKER seen video, ready to start!	COLLEGE PROFESSOR seen video, has questions
NAME	JILL JONES	DIANA HENDERSON
PHONE #	(123) 456-7890	(123) 456-7890
INFO (Seen video, product, occupation)	STOCK BROKER seen video, sell on potential	HOUSEWIFE seen products, ready to go!

(Left margin vertical label: PROSPECTS)

- List your distributors top 3 prospects.

- List the phone number where they're most likely to be reached.

- Call prospects as soon as possible and relay their response back to your distributor.

- Share your success stories with the prospects.

EXAMPLE OF
TOP 40
DISTRIBUTORS

SPONSORED DISTRIBUTOR	JAY EDWARDS	LORI THOMAS
NAME	**BILL BROWN**	**KAY LEWIS**
PHONE #s	(123) 456-7890 W 765-4321	(123) 456-7890 W 765-4321
INFO (Goals, Income Level, Titles)	Goals - 10 new recruits Full time in next 6 months	Goals - 5 sales weekly 5 new recruits monthly
NAME	**SALLY THOMPSON**	**STEVE MOORE**
PHONE #s	(123) 456-7890 W 765-4321	(123) 456-7890 W 765-4321
INFO (Goals, Income Level, Title)	Goals - $10,000 volume in 60 days	Goals - $15,000 in group sales next month
NAME	**TOM SIMPSON**	**BRENDA WILSON**
PHONE #s	(123) 456-7890 W 765-4321	(123) 456-7890 W 765-4321
INFO (Goals, Income Level, Title)	Goals - 3 fulltime distributors next 60 days	Goals - top position in company - $10K monthly income

KEY DISTRIBUTORS

- List your top ten distributors and their top three producers.
- List both home and work phone numbers.
- Keep important information on your producers to help you build and to track your organizations growth.
- Transfer to a "key leaders" page as each distributors' group develops.

TOP TEN PROSPECTS

NAME	DAY/NIGHT PHONE #'s	ADDRESS

1. _____ _____ _____

2. _____ _____ _____

3. _____ _____ _____

4. _____ _____ _____

5. _____ _____ _____

6. _____ _____ _____

7. _____ _____ _____

8. _____ _____ _____

9. _____ _____ _____

10. _____ _____ _____

* **Select this list from your "Who Do You Know " list.**

* **Once signed, transfer to "Top Ten Distributors" and/or "Top Ten Distributor's Prospects".**

* **Update list every 3-6 weeks.**

PRODUCT DEMO	VIDEO PACKET SENT	SEEN VIDEO	ATTENDED MEETING	FOLLOW-UP PHONE CALL	FOLLOW-UP MEETING WITH SPONSOR	COMPLETED APPLICATION	INITIAL ORDER	COMPLETED "WHO DO YOU KNOW" LIST	

TOP TEN DISTRIBUTORS

NAME	DAY/NIGHT PHONE #'s	ADDRESS
1.		
2.		
3.		
4.		
5.		
6.		
7.		
8.		
9.		
10.		

* Track Distributor growth with "Top 40" list.

* Update list every 6-8 weeks.

SS # / DIST. #	INITIAL ORDER	TITLE	MONTHLY INCOME GOAL	COMPLETED FOCUSING-IN STEPS	SIGNED 3-4	KEY PEOPLE

TOP TEN'S
PROSPECTS

DISTRIBUTOR

P R O S P E C T S

NAME
PHONE #
INFO
(seen video, product, occupation)

NAME
PHONE #
INFO
(seen video, product, occupation)

NAME
PHONE #
INFO
(seen video, product, occupation)

DISTRIBUTOR

P R O S P E C T S

NAME
PHONE #
INFO
(seen video, product, occupation)

NAME
PHONE #
INFO
(seen video, product, occupation)

NAME
PHONE #
INFO
(seen video, product, occupation)

* Transfer signed names to "Top 40 List" or "Leaders" page.

* Update list every 2-3 weeks.

TOP 40 DISTRIBUTORS

KEY DISTRIBUTORS

SPONSORED DISTRIBUTOR

NAME

PHONE #

INFO
(Goals, Income Level, Title)

NAME

PHONE #

INFO
(Goals, Income Level, Title)

NAME

PHONE #

INFO
(Goals, Income Level, Title)

KEY DISTRIBUTORS

SPONSORED DISTRIBUTOR

NAME

PHONE #

INFO
(Goals, Income Level, Title)

NAME

PHONE #

INFO
(Goals, Income Level, Title)

NAME

PHONE #

INFO
(Goals, Income Level, Title)

* Begin "Leaders" page once distributor has signed 3-4 key people.

* **Update list every 6-8 weeks.**

EXAMPLE OF
KEY LEADERS

Leaders Name	Address	Phone #	SS/Dist. #
Bill Smith	123 Bay Ave.	(123)456-7890	#12345

Sponsor	Distributor	Address	Phone #	SS/Dist. #
(BS)	Jim Carroll	111 Main	987-6543	#98765
(BS)	Bob Jones	111 Main	987-6543	#98765
BJ	Terri Ellis	111 Main	987-6543	#98765
TE	Sally Potter	111 Main	987-6543	#98765
SP	Bart Thomas	111 Main	987-6543	#98765
BJ	Don Wilson	111 Main	987-6543	#98765
TE	Paul Rote	111 Main	987-6543	#98765
(BS)	Jay Edwards	111 Main	987-6543	#98765
BJ	Kim Rawls	111 Main	987-6543	#98765
KR	Tony Cash	111 Main	987-6543	#98765
(BS)	Paula Mills	111 Main	987-6543	#98765
PM	Diane Hill	111 Main	987-6543	#98765
PM	Ed Taylor	111 Main	987-6543	#98765
(BS)	Helen Smith	111 Main	987-6543	#98765

(BS) Denotes Bill Smith's personally sponsored distributors

KEY LEADERS

Leaders Name	Address	Phone #	SS/Dist. #

Sponsor	Distributor	Address	Phone #	SS/Dist. #

$50.^{oo}
for a moment of your time!

Congratulations on Your Purchase!

Should you want to suggest others that will benefit from our products, please fill out this referral card. For each sale through your referral, you will receive $10 in appreciation. This offer is valid only 30 days from purchase date, so please fill it out today!

Your Name_____

Address_____

City_____Zip_____

Phone #_____

Products purchased_____

_____

Comments_____

_____

REFERRALS

Name_____

Address_____

City_____Zip_____

Phone #_____

Comments_____

_____

_____

REFERRALS

Name_____

Address_____

City_____Zip_____

Phone #_____

Comments_____

_____

_____

Name_____

Address_____

City_____Zip_____

Phone #_____

Comments_____

_____

_____

Name_____

Address_____

City_____Zip_____

Phone #_____

Comments_____

_____

_____

Name_____

Address_____

City_____Zip_____

Phone #_____

Comments_____

_____

_____

SAMPLE REFERRAL BROCHURE

YOUR NAME
ADDRESS
PHONE #

YOUR
COMPANY
NAME

OUTSIDE

INSIDE

$50.⁰⁰

**for a moment
of your time!**

**Congratulations on
Your Purchase!**

Should you want to suggest otl
ers that will benefit from our p
ducts, please fill out this referr
card. For each sale through yo
referral, you will receive $10 ii
appreciation. This offer is vali

REFERRALS

Same text as brochure
on opposite page

EXAMPLE OF
REFERRAL
LIST

	YOUR CONTACT	THEIR REFERRAL	PHONE #	ADDRESS	CONTACT WILL NOTIFY I'LL BE CALLING	RETAIL	BUSINESS	CONTACTED	FOLLOW-UP	RESULTS
1.	Bob Brown	Tim Jones	123-4567	123 Bay Ave.	√	√		√	√	sold
2.	Sally Evans	Mary Simm	123-4567	123 Bay Ave.	√	√		√	√	sold
3.	Tom Wilson	John Smith	123-4567	123 Bay Ave.	√		√	√	√	signed
4.	Linda Owens	Holly Martin	123-4567	123 Bay Ave.	√		√	√	√	not int.

REFERRAL LIST

YOUR CONTACT	THEIR REFERRAL	PHONE #	ADDRESS	CONTACT WILL NOTIFY / I'LL BE CALLING	RETAIL	BUSINESS	CONTACTED	FOLLOW-UP	RESULTS
1.									
2.									
3.									
4.									
5.									
6.									
7.									
8.									
9.									
10.									

DEBT FREE
LIST

TO BE DEBT FREE I NEED TO:	AMOUNT NEEDED	TIME NEEDED TO REACH GOAL
-Pay off my mortgage.	$_____	_____
-Pay off credit cards.	$_____	_____
-Pay off car notes.	$_____	_____
-Pay off bank/personal loans.	$_____	_____
-Pay cash for material needs (furniture, clothing, etc.).	$_____	_____
TOTAL DEBT	$_____	_____

Projected time needed to become completely debt free

_____years_____months.

Things I want to do once I become debt free and have more net cash to spend.

	AMOUNT DESIRED	TIME NEEDED TO REACH GOAL
Fund savings account	$_____	_____
College Fund for children	$_____	_____
Fund my own ministry / community projects	$_____	_____
Pay cash for _____	$_____	_____
Pay cash for a vacation to _____	$_____	_____
_____	$_____	_____
_____	$_____	_____

REMEMBER THIS IS A LONG TERM LIST!

"MY VISION"

My overall desire in life is _____

_____

_____

My top three goals for my family are:

#1._____

#2._____

#3._____

My top three financial goals are:

#1._____

#2._____

#3._____

My top three social goals are:

#1._____

#2._____

#3._____

My top three ministry / charity goals are:

#1._____

#2._____

#3._____

My top three individual goals are:

#1._____

#2._____

#3._____

When I get to be financially free, I want to: _____

_____

_____

A FINAL NOTE

- Study the book. Use it as a personal reference manual.

- Teach your group the principles outlined in this book. Use it as a training manual.

- Review, complete and use the worksheets.

- Impliment the Action Points.

> *"When you want a thing deeply, earnestly and intensely, this feeling of desire reinforces your will and arouses in you the determination to work for the desired object. When you have a distinct purpose in view, your work becomes of absorbing interest. You bend your best powers to it; you give it concentrated attention; you think of little else than the realization of this purpose; your will is stimulated into unusual activity, and as a consequence, you do your work with an increasing sense of power."*
>
> *- Grenville Kleiser*

RECOMMENDED READING

Adler, Mortimer J. *How to Speak, How to Listen*. New York: Macmillan Publishing Company, Inc., 1983.

Ash, Mary Kay. *Mary Kay on People Management*. New York: Warner Books, 1984.

Bennis, Warren, and Burt Nanus. *Leaders: The Strategies for Taking Charge*. New York: Harper and Row, 1985.

Blue, Ron. *Master Your Money*. Nashville, Tennessee: Thomas Nelson, Inc., 1986.

Carnegie, Dale and Associates. *Managing Through People*. New York: Simon & Schuster, Inc., 1978.

Carnegie, Dale. *How to Stop Worrying and Start Living*. New York: Simon & Schuster, Inc., 1975.

Clason, George S. *The Richest Man in Babylon*. New York: Hawthorn Books, 1955.

Cook, James R. *The Start-Up Entrepreneur*. New York: E.P. Dutton, 1987.

DeBono, Edward. *Tactics: The Art and Science of Success*. Boston: Little Brown, 1984.

DeBruyn, Robert I. *Causing Others to Want Your Leadership*. Manhattan, Kansas: DeBruyn & Associates, 1976.

Flesch, Rudolph. *How to Write, Speak, and Think More Effectively.* New York: The New American Library of World Literature, Inc. , Signet Books, 1960.

Fooshee, George Jr. *You Can Be Financially Free.* Old Tappan, N.J.: Revell, 1976.

_____ and Marjean Fooshee. *You Can Beat the Money Squeeze.* Old Tappan, N.J.: Revell, 1980.

Garfield, Charles A. *Peak Performance.* Boston: Houghton Mifflin Company, 1984.

Gschwandtner, Gerhard. *Superachievers.* Englewood Cliffs, New Jersey: Prentice-Hall, Inc., 1984.

Harvey, Paul. *The Rest of the Story...*Compiled by Lynne Harvey. Chicago: Paulynne, Inc., 1969.

Hayes, Ira. *Yak! Yak! Yak!* Ira M. Hayes, 1978.

Hunsaker, Phillip L. and Anthony J. Alessandra. *The Art of Managing People.* Englewood Cliffs, New Jersey: Prentice-Hall, Inc., 1980.

Iacocca, Lee. *Iacocca: An Autobiography.* New York: Bantam Books, 1984.

Jones, Charlie. *Life Is Tremendous.* Wheaton, Illinois: Tyndale House, 1981.

Kami, Michael J. *Trigger Points.* New York: McGraw-Hill Book Company, 1988.

Kinzel, Robert K. *Retirement.* New York: AMACOM, 1979.

Levinson, H. and S. Rosenthal . *CEO: Corporate Leadership in Action.* New York: Basic Books, 1984.

McCormack, Mark H. *What They Don't Teach You at Harvard Business*

School. New York: Bantam Books, 1984.

Meyer, Paul J. *Dynamics of Goal Setting.* Waco, Texas: Success Motivation Institute, 1977. Lesson manual, cassette tapes and plan of action.

_____. *Dynamics of Personal Motivation.* Third Edition. Waco, Texas: Success Motivation Institute, 1983. A kit consisting of: "Lesson Manual," "Cassette Tapes," and "A Plan of Action"

Montgomery, Field-Marshal. *Path to Leadership.* New York: G.T. Putman and Sons, 1961.

Naisbitt, John. *Megatrends: Ten New Directions Transforming Our Lives.* New York: Warner Books, 1982.

_____. and Patricia Aburdene. *Megatrends 2000.* New York: William Morrow and Company, Inc., 1990.

Otto, Herbert A. *Guide to Developing Your Potential.* New York: Charles Scribners Sons, 1957.

"Paths Toward Personal Progress: Leaders are Made, Not Born." Harvard Business Review , 1980.

Peters, Thomas J. and Robert H. Waterman, Jr. *In Search of Excellence.* New York: Harper & Row, Publishers, 1982.

_____. and Nancy K. Austin. *A Passion for Excellence.* New York: Random House, 1985.

Peters, Tom. *Thriving on Chaos.* New York: Alfred A. Knopf, 1987.

Sarnoff, Dorothy. *Speech Can Change Your Life.* New York: Dell Publishing company, 1970.

Smith, Fred. *Learning to Lead.* Waco, Texas: Word Books, 1986.

Stillman, Richard J. *Guide to Personal Finance: A Lifetime Program of Money Management.* Englewood Cliffs, N.J.: Prentice-Hall, 1979.

Swindoll, Charles R. *Leadership.* Waco: Word Books, Publisher, 1985.

Taylor, Robert Lewis. *Winston Churchill*. New York: Pocket Books, Inc. 1952.

Thoughts on the Business Life. New York: B.C. Forbes & Sons Publishing Co., Inc., 1950.

Thoughts on the Business Life II. New York: B.C. Forbes & Sons Publishing Co., Inc., 1984.

Waitley, Denis. *The Winner's Edge: the Critical Attitude of Success*. New York: Times Books, 1980.

_____. *Seeds Of Greatness*. Old Tappan, New Jersey: Fleming H. Revell Company, 1983.

_____. and Robert B. Tucker. *Winning the Innovation Game*. Old Tappan, N.J.: Revell, 1986.

Williamson, Porter B. *Patton's Principles*. New York: Simon and Schuster, 1979.

Ziglar, Zig. *See You at the Top*. Gretna, Louisiana: Pelican, 1985.

_____. *Top Performance*. Old Tappan, New Jersey: Fleming H. Revell Company, 1986.

_____. *Zig Ziglar's Secrets of Closing the Sale*. Old Tappan, New Jersey: Fleming H. Revell Company, 1984.

Continued Education

American Demographics. Published monthly by American Demographics, Inc., 108 North Cayuga Street, Ithaca, N.Y. 14850.

Bits & Pieces. Published monthly by Economics Press, Inc., 12 Daniel Road, Fairfield, New Jersey 07006.

Decker Communications Report. Published monthly by Magna Publications, Inc., 607 N. Sherman Avenue, Madison, Wisconsin 53704.

Entrepreneur. Published monthly by Entreprenuer Group, Inc., 2311 Pontius Avenue, Los Angeles, California 90064.

Harvard Business Review. Published monthly by Harvard Business Review, Soldiers Field, Boston, Massachusetts 02163.

Money Makers Monthly. Published monthly by the Multi-Level Marketing International Association, P.O. Box 7116, Villa Park Illinois 60181.

National Speakers Association. 4323 N. 12th Street, Suite 103, Phoenix, Arizona 85014.

Performax Systems International, Inc. Personal Profile Systems, 3140 Harbor Lane North, Suite 200, Minneapolis, Minnesota 55441.

Personal Selling Power. Published monthly by Gerhard Gschwandtner & Associates, P.O. Box 5467, Fredericksburg, Virginia 22403.

Sales and Marketing Management. Published monthly by Bill Communications, Inc., 633 Third Avenue, New York, N.Y. 10017.

Selling by Phone. Published by Economics Press, Inc., Fairfield, New Jersey 07006.

Success. Published monthly by Success Unlimited, Inc,. P.O. box 2240 Boulder, Colorado 80322.

Working Smart. Published monthly by Learning International, P.O. Box 10211, Stamford, Connecticut 06904

SPECIALIZED MATERIAL

Trade and technical publications pertinent to the lines of business of the organization.

Functional publications (personnel, marketing, new product development) relating to the leader's main responsibilities.

INDEX

SUGGESTIONS

Document : Financially Free! The "HOW TO's" of Building a Large,
Successful Direct Sales / Network Marketing Organization.

Please suggest improvements to this book.

_____

_____

_____

_____

_____

Please list any errors in this book. Specify by page.

_____

_____

_____

_____

_____

Name_____ Title_____

Company_____

Address_____

_____

Date:_____ Business Phone No.:_____

FOR ORDERING INFORMATION

SEE PAGES 253-255

NOTES

NOTES

NOTES

NOTES

NOTES

NOTES

NOTES

NOTES

NOTES

NOTES

NOTES

FINANCIALLY FREE!
TRAINING AIDS

AUDIO / VIDEO
Versions of *FINANCIALLY FREE!* are
now available for individual or group/
wholesale purchase.

DAYTIMER INSERTS
Both 5 1/2" x 8 1/2" and 8 1/2" x 11 1/2" professionally
printed copies of all *FINANCIALLY FREE!* worksheets
are now available. These are a must for setting and
reaching your goals and tracking the growth of your organization! Also included are overviews of the key
points of this book to keep with you at all times!

For ordering information, contact:

WINDSOR INTERNATIONAL
P.O. BOX 850201
RICHARDSON, TEXAS 75085
(214) 644-7500

SEMINAR / SPEAKING INFORMATION

Dennis Windsor is available to help
your group reach their goals!

For information on:

FINANCIALLY FREE! Seminars
Keynote Addresses
Consulting Services

Contact:

WINDSOR INTERNATIONAL
P.O. BOX 850201
RICHARDSON, TEXAS 75085
(214) 644-7500

ORDERING INFORMATION

To obtain additional copies of
FINANCIALLY FREE! , call your
local bookstore or address:

WINDWARD PRESS
P.O. BOX 744275
DALLAS, TEXAS 75374

or contact:

WINDSOR INTERNATIONAL
P.O. BOX 850201
RICHARDSON, TEXAS 75085
(214) 644-7500